B.L. & R.L. DOLLEN

COLLECTOR BOOKS
A Division of Schroeder Publishing Co., Inc.

Searching For A Publisher?

Front cover:

Hearthstone Orange Single Candleholder. No bottom mark, orange, candleholder, $55.00 – 75.00.
Vase – #873 – 4½", semi-matte yellow, miniature vase, $55.00 – 70.00.
Planter. No bottom mark – 6½", matte blue, silver wing label, lamb planter, $110.00 – 145.00.
Vase. #B2005 – 8", gloss yellow/dark green, Shell ginger, Tropicana vase, $36.00 – 46.00.
Vase. #M1510 – 7", semi-matte coral/tan, long handled bud vase, $28.00 – 40.00.
Vase. 7", bottom stamped "Red Wing Art Pottery," dark green, cattail design Brushed Ware vase, $85.00 – 130.00.

Back cover:
Vase. #447 – 8", gloss coral/tan, Sylvan style vase, $65.00 – 80.00.
Bowl. #791 – 6½", gloss Persian blue/white, small bowl, $38.00 – 46.00.
Plain Pattern Swirl Pitcher. Unmarked – 64 oz., gloss royal blue/white, pitcher, $75.00 – 100.00

The Art Pottery in this book is from the author's collection unless otherwise noted.

Cover design by Beth Summers
Book design by Beth Ray

Additional copies of this book may be ordered from:

COLLECTOR BOOKS
P.O. Box 3009
Paducah, Kentucky 42002-3009

@$19.95. Add $2.00 for postage and handling.

Printed in the U.S.A. by Image Graphics, Paducah, KY

Contents

Dedication

Art Pottery by definition is any article created by a gifted artist, for beauty rather than utility, and can encompass even tableware....

This book is dedicated to all the people who are Red Wing collectors, and as you know, we appreciate the beauty of their fine pottery. Also, to those who will become collectors in the future and no doubt learn to appreciate it also.

Acknowledgments

I wish to express my appreciation for the help I received in researching Red Wing Art Pottery at the Goodhue County Historical Society Library, located in Red Wing, Minnesota. Also, for assistance at the research center of the Minnesota Historical Society, located in St. Paul, Minnesota.

Reference materials used at the Goodhue County Historical Society were:
Copies of original Red Wing Catalogs, dated 1930s through 1965,
Property of the Goodhue County Historical Society.

Reference materials used at the Minnesota Historical Society were:
Original Red Wing Catalogs, dated 1956 through 1966,
Property of the archives of the Minnesota Historical Society.

Special Acknowledgment

I would like to give a special thank you to Bev and Duane Brown who own and operate B & D Collectibles & Antiques, in Harlan, Iowa. Allowing me to photograph pieces from their collection contributed significantly to this book.

Photographs by Troy A. Petry

Pricing & Value Guide

The values included in this book are not meant to set prices. They are a general guide on pricing which can vary considerably due to demand and the area where the item is purchased. The price ranges in this book are an average of prices in different areas of the country. The pricing given assumes that the pottery is in very good condition. Cracks or chips take away from the value of art pottery. In turn, pieces in perfect condition command higher prices.

You may find some bargain prices at yard sales, auctions, and thrift stores. However people at thrift stores and auctions are now more knowledgeable about antiques, and you will find most of them separate the antiques and sell them at considerably higher prices than the other items.

You will also find some areas where the prices are considerably higher. This is a result of several factors. As a general guide for pricing, you will find this book's prices to be within the range of most Red Wing Art Pottery you will find.

Introduction

My first book, *Red Wing Art Pottery,* has been available since August 1996. I hope it has helped you look for and find some Red Wing Art Pottery. I'm sure some of you also got...Red Wing Fever.

If you have and are looking around quite a bit for Red Wing, you have no doubt noticed there were many different pieces of pottery produced by Red Wing. My first book gave you a good look at the art pottery, but by no means covers everything produced. There are hundreds of different pieces of Red Wing Art Pottery.

Since the first book, I have collected many new interesting pieces. There are many of us Red Wing people, and I have also had the opportunity to photograph pieces from others' collections. Some of both theirs and mine are unusual and rare items; all are different than the pottery in Book I.

I have prepared this second book to give you a broader look at Red Wing Art Pottery. This book gives you a whole new scope of pottery that you can look for and find. Both this second edition and my first book stand alone. You can use either to start collecting Red Wing, or both for a larger scope of the art pottery produced. Each book contains different pieces of art pottery.

As you can see, I still have Red Wing Fever — I am sure I always will. Hopefully after reading either the first or second edition, you will be excited enough to go out and look for some Red Wing Art Pottery. If you have a collection, check out your pieces in the books. If you do not have any Red Wing, look around and find a piece you like, purchase it, and check to see if you have found a rare item or perhaps a bargain.

The possibilities of what you can find are endless, as is the joy you will get from collecting.

About This Book

Since publication of *Red Wing Art Pottery,* I have had quite a few people who are not yet collectors ask me questions on how to use the book. Some thought they could purchase items from the book like a catalog. Other did not know where to buy Red Wing. Therefore, I thought it would be a good idea to explain the purpose of these books for those who are not familiar with collecting.

This book is an identification and value guide. It is meant to help you identify a piece of Red Wing Art Pottery and give you an average price you can expect to pay for the item. As stated in the Price Guide, these prices will vary.

Pieces of Red Wing Art Pottery are considered antiques. You will need to look in antique stores to find them. These can be individual stores or antique malls which have a number of dealers selling items in them.

Red Wing may also be available at some auctions and antiques sales. There are several monthly antique papers that you can get for a listing of sales and auctions.

You may look in several stores or go to several sales to find any Red Wing. Some auctions may have whole collections of Red Wing for sale. The larger auctions usually list what antiques will be available, so you will know before you attend.

Now that you have an idea where to look, you can read this book and pick out a piece you like. You will know the approximate price you will have to pay, and you can start looking for Red Wing Art Pottery.

Happy hunting!

History of Red Wing

In 1861 a German immigrant, Joseph Paul, settled on a farm near Red Wing, Minnesota. He soon discovered that the clays near the farm were excellent for making utilitarian wares such as crocks and churns. He started making these stoneware items in an old school house and sold them to the local citizens. Mr. Paul left the area around the time of the Civil War, but he is credited with discovering the clay around Red Wing.

In 1868 David Hallem began operating a stoneware pottery in his home in Red Wing. This venture was not successful and was eventually purchased by a group of citizens who formed a corporation under the name of Red Wing Stoneware Company. Mr. Hallem was the first to supervise this operation in 1878. The venture proved successful and Red Wing Stoneware Company was recognized as one of the leading producers of stoneware in the United States.

Soon two competitors entered the field, Minnesota Stoneware Company in 1883, and Northstar in 1892. After four years the Northstar Company closed. In the early 1900s both Red Wing Stoneware Company and Minnesota Stoneware Company burned. After constructing new plants, the two companies merged forming Red Wing Union Stoneware Company. They later introduced a pottery line in addition to the stoneware line; eventually the company created an art ware line. The Brushed Ware Line was the first decorative art ware introduced in the late 1920s. In 1930 they introduced the Glazed Ware art pottery lines with fine smooth glazes and classic shapes.

The name of the pottery was changed in 1936 from Red Wing Union Stoneware Company to Red Wing Potteries Inc. Sometime in the early 1930s, Red Wing contracted to produce a line of art pottery for a marketing agent in Little Rock, Arkansas, named George Rumrill. Mr. Rumrill designed a lot of the items in this line and it was named after him. They continued to produce RumRill until 1938 when he ceased purchasing from Red Wing. Mr. Rumrill then contracted with Eastern potteries to produce his wares.

Red Wing discontinued the stoneware line in 1947 and continued to produce the art pottery lines until 1967 when labor problems and a dwindling market forced them to close their doors. Red Wing Pottery had been producing their wares for 89 years at the time they closed.

The remaining stock was sold, piece by piece, at a salesroom across the street from the pottery. A legend in their field, Red Wing Pottery will never be forgotten.

History Chart

1878 ....Red Wing Union Stoneware Company

1883 ....Minnesota Stoneware Company
(competitor)

1892 ....Northstar Company
(competitor)

1896 ....Northstar Company out of business

1900 ....Minnesota Stoneware Company burns
(Spring)

1900 ....Red Wing Union Stoneware burns
(Fall)
(Both companies rebuild and merge)

1908 ....Red Wing Union Stoneware Company
(Official reincorporating)
(Trademark RED WING)

1929 ....Introduced Art Ware line

1930 ....Introduced Fine Art Pottery line

1935 ....Introduced Dinnerware line

1936 ....Red Wing Potteries
(Legal name change)

1947 ....Ceased production of stoneware

1967 ....Plant closed

Preface

The art pottery line of Red Wing was first introduced in the 1920s with the Brushed Ware line. The pottery was a crude line using the same clay they used to make the Stoneware line, with some modifications.

Glazed Ware art pottery was added. In the 1930s due to a decrease in the market for the Stoneware line and because they were running out of local clay, they hired Belle Kogan, a New York designer, to create a line of fine art pottery. This line required blended earthen clays, which they imported from other states.

These early lines of art pottery created in the 1930s were very ornate, each having distinctive handles and base decorations that matched their names. They are also very hard to find. Belle Kogan created many of the decorative early lines, among them the popular Magnolia line. She also created the Renaissance and Vintage lines. Another designer, George Murphy, is credited with designing distinctive art ware and dinnerware.

They later simplified and standardized the early lines, some of which were carried throughout the 1950s and 1960s. Eva Zeisel, another New York designer, created other art ware and the Town and Country Dinnerware line introduced in 1946.

Glazes on the art ware consisted of soft velvety matte, semi-matte, and gloss, produced in an array of colors. The art pottery was also marked on the bottom with the Red Wing name and numbered. These numbers were shape numbers used also as catalog numbers. The early Brushed Ware line and Glaze Ware had stamped markings, and the later '30s art pottery had the marking inscribed on the bottom. You will find color charts and pictures of bottom markings in the back of this book.

Wing stamps were placed on some of the art pottery produced. These stamps were done in gold, silver, and also red. Since they were placed on random pieces, you will not find a lot of pottery that displays these stamps. But, found in tact, they can increase the value of the item up to $10.00 – $15.00, depending on the condition of pottery itself. There are also pictures of these wing stamps in the back of the book.

This information gives you an idea of what to look for on Red Wing art pottery. There is a chapter on "Learning About Red Wing Pottery" in my first book *Red Wing Art Pottery*. This chapter gives you complete details, along with pictures, on how to identify art pottery.

Collecting Red Wing Pottery

Why Collect

There is a variety of reasons why and how people collect Red Wing Art Pottery, and also a difference between collectors. I am sure there is a category you will fit into among them.

Some collect a few pieces that simply caught their eye. These collectors use the items in their homes. They put flowers in the vases, display fruit or other things in the bowls, and use the candleholders with candles that match their decor. Their collection is strictly for personal enjoyment.

The next category is the serious collector, who purchases many pieces of Red Wing Art Pottery and owns a large collection which can consist of several hundred pieces. These collectors are usually looking at their collection as an investment. They have collected for many years, and therefore have purchased a lot of the pieces at prices that are lower than today's value. As Red Wing Art Pottery increases in popularity, the future prices can be higher than they are today. Red Wing Art Pottery is fast becoming one of the hot collectibles in today's market. Therefore, a collection can increase in value over time and can be worth considerably more than the purchase price, making it not only a good investment, but also giving you some quality pieces to display in the home.

Still another category is the collectors somewhere in between who purchase Red Wing pottery for resale. They are constantly buying and selling their items. Often they rent a booth in one of the many antique malls throughout the U.S. and make a profit on their Red Wing purchases.

How people collect is often done according to the reason why they collect. The serious collector usually purchases any Red Wing art ware not in their collection, and some purchase duplicate pieces. The resale collector will purchase any art ware they find that is priced within their price range, that would allow for a mark-up at the time of sale. Those collecting to display often purchase the art ware that catches their eye or is a color they want for their decor.

As Is Art Pottery

Whatever your reason for collecting, there is one thing you will need to remember. Any damage such as cracks or chips on an item reduces the value of the piece considerably, no matter how small. You will find that you can get some bargain prices on art pottery sold *As Is*. Most damaged pottery will be marked as such, but you will need to examine the piece even if it is not marked *"As Is,"* in case the seller overlooked the damage.

If you are collecting simply to display the art pottery in your home, this will not be as big a factor to you, and by purchasing damaged pieces you will not have to make as large of an investment. However, if you are purchasing as an investment or for resale, this can greatly reduce your amount of profit.

Ways to Organize a Collection

There are numerous ways a collection can be organized. A few of these are item, color, specific line, for display, novelty pieces, and miniatures.

Collecting by item can be done in several different ways. You can have a whole collection consisting of different pieces of one item, such as vases. This could also be done with any of the art pottery, such as bowls, planters, candleholders, or numerous other items. Arranging a collection of one item in different colors also works out very well. Red Wing produced many shapes that were each finished in a wide array of colors. A good example for this collection is vase #505 shown in the miscellaneous group of the RumRill section. This shape was also produced in the Red Wing line in a multitude of beautiful colors, such as the one shown in the 1950s section. Another example is the fan vase #892 shown in the Floraline section of the 1960s art pottery. This vase also was produced in many lovely colors. Any of these examples would be a collection anyone would be proud to own, and would give a beautiful display.

Color is another very good way to organize your collection. This can be accomplished by purchasing different pieces of art pottery all with the same color finish. Since the colors in the finishes used by Red Wing were produced over and over, there are many of the colors that you could find that would give you a wide array of different items. A good example of this is the Luster Blue/Coral finish. You will find vase #1160 in the 1940s section which shows this color. There are more examples of this finish throughout the book. The fleck colors would also make a great collection. Vase #M1457 in the 1950s section shows an example of the fleck yellow finish. There is also fleck Nile blue, fleck zephyr pink, and fleck green, which you will see throughout the book. Other colors that would be good for this type of collection are white, black, blue, and a combination of black and white items. Any of these colors makes a very elegant collection.

A collection by *specific line* works very well. Magnolia is one very good example of this type of organization. You will see example of Magnolia in the 1920s and 1930s section. There were also novelty pieces produced in the Magnolia such as a small box and a small ashtray, which would make a Magnolia collection very diverse. Brushed Ware would also make an excellent collection; although not as colorful as the others, it would be a valuable collection since it was the first art pottery produced by Red Wing. Another valuable and also colorful collection would be RumRill. These specific line collections would be ones that any other collector would envy. However, you will find them to be more expensive than some of the other collections and also harder to find.

Novelty pieces also make a fun collection. Red Wing produced many different kinds of novelty planters, such as deer, giraffe, donkey, swan, rabbit, owl, and dachshund. A collection of these items would be very novel. Again these items are harder to find and more expensive, but the effort to gather a collection would be worthwhile.

If your display space is limited, collecting *miniatures* is a good way to handle that. Red Wing produced a number of miniature vases and planters. These are quite hard to find and also quite expensive; however the results are not only ornate, but since they are scarce, it would be a very valuable collection.

Looking for specific items to purchase, such as these suggested, will take some time. But as we collectors know, the hunt is a large part of the fun. And when complete, collections such as these will be very pleasing.

Throughout the book you will find items noted for particular collections. However, the possibilities are limited only to your imagination. Red Wing Art Pottery has a look of quality that enhances any setting in which it is placed. No matter how your collection is organized or what your reason is for collecting, you will be able to find many places in your home to display your Red Wing.

Art Pottery Displays

Several examples of how Red Wing art pottery can be displayed follow. You can be sure that anyone collecting is also displaying some of their art ware.

Many different pottery pieces can be displayed on a dining room table and will add charm to your home. Below is an example of this, with a display from the Magnolia line of Red Wing.

MAGNOLIA LINE DISPLAY: Magnolia Vase. #1030 – 9", $70.00 – 90.00. Magnolia Candleholders, #1228 – 4½", $22.00 – 30.00 each. These pieces are all finished in the ivory/brown wipe method.

A piano display gives a very elegant look to your music room. Below the piano is displayed with a Red Wing violin planter along with a RumRill vase. Red Wing also made a banjo and a small piano in the music line planters.

RED WING VIOLIN PLANTER & RUMRILL VASE: Violin Wall Planter, #1484 – 13", semi-matte black, $48.00 – 58.00. RumRill Vase #641 – 7", matte aqua/gloss white, $56.00 – 70.00.

A replica of an antique wash stand displays almost any piece of pottery exquisitely. At right are a Red Wing Vintage Line pitcher vase and candleholders in lieu of a bowl and pitcher.

VINTAGE LINE PITCHER VASE & CANDLEHOLDERS: Vintage Pitcher Vase, #616 – 11", semi-matte ivory/brown wipe, $145.00 – 225.00. Vintage Candleholders, #622 – 5½", semi-matte ivory/brown wipe, $48.00 – 64.00 pair.

Displayed on a buffet is a Red Wing Deluxe line console set. As you can see, this set adds color and warmth to the room, and accents the picture in the background.

RED WING DELUXE LINE CONSOLE SET: Deluxe Line Ivy Bowl, #B2504 – 14½", gloss green, $85.00 – 110.00. Deluxe Line Swan Figurine, #B2506 – 9", gloss green, $95.00 – 125.00, Deluxe Line Ivy Candlesticks, B2505 – 4½", gloss green, $45.00 – 60.00 pair.

A group of vases on a marble top table add the touch of color you need for any room. The table below displays Red Wing and RumRill vases.

RED WING & RUMRILL VASES: Center front clockwise, Red Wing Miniature Vase, #873 – 4½", semi-matte yellow, $55.00 – 68.00. RumRill Vase, #291 – 5½", semi-matte ocean green, $55.00 – 72.00. Red Wing Chromoline Vase, #637 – 8", gloss blue/yellow combination, $85.00 – 98.00. RumRill Vase, #500 – 5½", semi-matte Dutch blue/stipple, $75.00 – 90.00.

Collecting Miniatures

Even if you do not have an antique setting in your home, Red Wing looks just as elegant on any type of furniture.

The smaller collections such as miniatures or novelty planters can be displayed on a shelf in a hutch, a hanging shelf on a wall, or on an occasional table.

The picture below shows a small display of Red Wing on one shelf of a hutch. You can put quite a few pieces in that limited space. The picture has been taken with the door open to avoid reflection, but the display shows perfectly with the door closed.

When collecting miniatures, you will find they are higher in price than some of the other art pottery, due to the fact they are scarce.

RED WING MINIATURE & SMALL NOVELTY PIECES: Center front clockwise, Magnolia Ashtray, #1019 – 4½", semi-matte ivory/brown wipe, $42.00 – 56.00. Lamb Planter, #1343 – 6½", semi-matte blue, $110.00 – 125.00. Miniature Vase, #873 – 4½", semi-matte yellow, $55.00 – 70.00. Shoe Vase, #651 – 6½", semi-matte ivory, $115.00 – 140.00. Red Wing Collectors Society 1996 Commemorative, $75.00 – 85.00. Although the colors do not show very well inside the hutch, it gives you an idea of how many items you can put on a small shelf.

Water Coolers

Other collections of Red Wing you might consider are the dinnerware, cookie jars, or water coolers. The dinnerware was produced in many lovely patterns, some of which can be seen on pages 114 – 153. Dinnerware can be displayed in a hutch or around the top of the kitchen on a shelf. You can also set a beautiful table with an entire dinnerware set of the same pattern. The cookie jar or water cooler could be used as a functional item in the kitchen.

Red Wing water coolers were produced in many of the dinnerware patterns. A collection of coolers is quite an accomplishment since they are scarce and very expensive. It would, however, be unique and quite valuable.

The water cooler below shows that a pleasant touch is added to the kitchen where a cooler is used to dispense water.

Red Wing Water Cooler: Tampico 2-gallon water cooler with stand, $600.00 – 750.00. From the collection of Bev and Duane Brown.

Cookie Jars

Red Wing produced many types of cookie jars; quite a number of them matched a dinnerware pattern. Others were shaped like fruit, and some were characters. There was a girl called the Katrina, Pierre the Chef, and the King of Tarts among others. The King of Tarts is a much sought after piece. Prices can range up to $900.00 for this cookie jar, which looks like a court jester.

The cookie jar pictured below shows how these pieces add charm to a kitchen counter. Collecting Red Wing cookie jars makes a very interesting collection.

Red Wing Friar Tuck Cookie Jar: Bottom stamped "Red Wing Pottery Hand Painted," yellow with brown accents, $110.00 – 160.00 in very good condition. This cookie jar has two bottom markings; the other reads Red Wing USA inscribed under the glaze.

Whether you display your Red Wing in some of the above manners or in you own style, there is no doubt you can find Red Wing Art Pottery in a color or type suited to your decor.

The numerous different pieces of Red Wing Art Pottery that were produced make it easy to find some that will fit your situation. With a little imagination, there is a collection suited to everyone. Use your imagination along with this book, and go collect.

Art Pottery – 1920s & 1930s

Brushed Ware Line

The Brushed Ware line was the first art pottery produced by Red Wing. Introduced in the 1920s, it was made with the same clay used for the stoneware, with some modifications. It was a rustic line, decorated with acorns, cranes, cattails, flowers, and leaves. Red Wing had been producing flowerpots in the same designs prior to the introduction of the art pottery vases.

George Hehr designed the first art pottery vases. Bowls, urns, jardinieres, and other vases, along with some specialty pieces, were later added to the line. All the pieces were a rustic design with stain brushed over a tan body. The colors of the stain were dark green, light green, bronze tan, and luster green. The inside of the pottery was covered in a luster glaze usually of the same color used on the outside.

While crude, Brushed Ware holds a special place in the history of the art pottery lines and in the hearts of collectors. It was the beginning of a pottery legend, the oldest line of Red Wing Art Pottery. Though not as refined as its later fine art pottery counterparts, it has a quality look that definitely fits the category of antique. A collection of Brushed Ware would be unique; you would own the items that were the beginning of an art pottery legend.

The art pottery in this chapter is from the author's collection, unless otherwise noted.

VASE. 7", bottom stamped "Red Wing Art Pottery," dark green, cattail design Brushed Ware vase, $ 85.00 – 130.00. You could also purchase a tan stone flower-frog insert for these vases. Although rarely found with the insert the pricing is higher, $125.00 – 150.00. The rough look of this vase indicates that perhaps it was one the first Brushed Ware items. Even the inside glaze is not as refined as some of the other Brushed Ware pieces.

VASE. 7", bottom stamped "Red Wing Art Pottery," bronze tan, swirl Brushed Ware vase, $65.00 – 90.00. The finish on this vase has a sand like texture.

VASE. 7", bottom stamped "Red Wing Union Stoneware Co.," dark green, acorn design Brushed Ware Cleveland Style Vase, $85.00 – 110.00.

A vase like the one above, except with lion head handles and additional colors, was presented to Mrs. Grover Cleveland when she and her husband visited Red Wing. The vase had her name and date inscribed around the rim. Copies of the vase with some variations were later mass-produced and became known as the Cleveland.

VASE. 8", bottom stamped "Red Wing Union Stoneware Co.," blue green, cactus flower design Brushed Ware vase, $95.00 – 120.00. The blue green Brushed Ware is quite hard to find and commands higher prices. Most of the Brushed Ware found is in the dark green color. From the collection of Bev & Duane Brown.

You can tell by looking at the Brushed Ware pieces that they were made from the same crude clay as the stoneware. The color stain was fired on the art ware and gives a soft pastel look.

BOWL. 9½", bottom stamped "Red Wing Art Pottery," dark green leaf design Brushed Ware bulb bowl, $95.00 – 135.00. These bowls were used to plant indoor flowers grown from bulbs, such as tulips or daffodils, and were referred to as bulb bowls. From the collection of Bev & Duane Brown.

FLOWER POT WITH BOTTOM SAUCER. 9", bottom stamped "Red Wing Union Stoneware Co.," dark green, leaf design Brushed Ware flowerpot with Saucer, 10" diameter, also bottom stamped, dark green, Set $140.00 – 175.00. This flowerpot was also sold without the saucer. Flowerpots alone $95.00 – 135.00. These flowerpots, made for greenhouse use, were the first items produced after the stoneware sales dwindled in 1922.

PITCHER. No bottom mark, dark green, Rustic Brushed Ware pitcher, $150.00 – 185.00. There are mugs to match this pitcher. With no handles they look more like glasses, but were known as mugs in the Red Wing catalog.

Glazed Ware

Glazed Ware was the next art pottery introduced by Red Wing. Vases were the first items produced; they were plain Egyptian style art ware, produced in semi-matte glazes of clear bright greens, yellows, blues, and maroons. Later the Glazed Ware included various shaped vases, bowls, urns, planters, candlesticks, and some novelty items. The colors included the ones listed above and some combination colors. There is a list of some of the early Glazed Ware colors in the back of the book.

Quite scarce, these early Glazed Ware pieces command high prices, again because they are some of the oldest Red Wing Art Pottery and difficult to find. You will also notice that in spite of being the first glazed art ware produced by Red Wing using unrefined techniques, the pieces are quite beautiful. They have the look of something produced in a later era.

Red Wing continued to sell the Brushed Ware line along with the glazed art ware, giving each separate pages and price lists in the catalogs. Most of the Brushed Ware was bottom stamped only. The early Glazed Ware was bottom stamped with the same marking, but was also engraved with a shape number. Examples are shown in the bottom marking section at the end of this book.

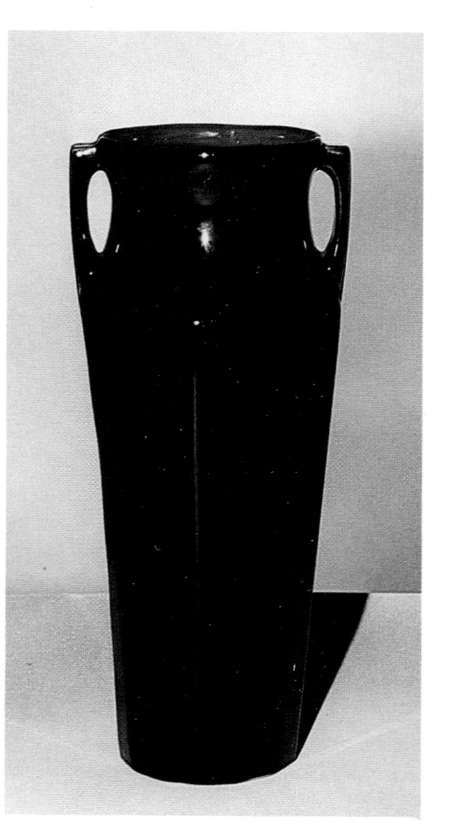

Vase. #154 – 12", bottom stamped "Red Wing Art Pottery Co.," dark blue, Egyptian vase, $145.00 – 165.00. This blue is so dark that it looks almost black except in very good light. Advertised in the Red Wing price list as dark blue or blue black, this color commands higher prices than the other colors. The maroon color also carries a higher price. From the collection of Bev & Duane Brown.

Vase. #154 – 12", bottom stamped "Red Wing Art Pottery," semi-matte light green, Egyptian vase, $110.00 – 135.00. From the collection of Bev & Duane Brown.

Vase. #158 – 15", bottom stamped "Red Wing Art Pottery," gloss white/green, Egyptian vase, $125.00 – 150.00. Styled like the first Egyptian vase pictured earlier. From the collection of Bev & Duane Brown.

Vase. #158 – 12", bottom stamped "Red Wing Art Pottery," gloss white/green, Egyptian vase, $110.00 – 135.00. From the collection of Bev & Duane Brown.

Vase. #157 – 12", bottom stamped "Red Wing Art Pottery," gloss green/white, Egyptian vase, $110.00 – 135.00. This is the same style vase as the previous ones, done in a different pattern and with colors reversed.

Jugs. 8¾", bottom stamped "Red Wing Art Pottery," gloss blue, genie type jugs, $225.00 – 260.00 each. Some of the first Glazed Ware pottery, the jug came with a stopper in the same glaze and color as the jug. With stopper, $250.00 – 300.00 each. Perhaps used to water flowers, these jugs are quite beautiful. From the collection of Bev & Duane Brown.

Fine Art Pottery Lines

The Fine Art Pottery of Red Wing, which is also glazed ware, was produced starting in the 1930s. Due to a decrease in the market for the Stoneware line and because they were running out of the local clay they used, Red Wing hired designers Belle Kogan, Charles Murphy, and Eva Zeisel. They designed much of the early Fine Art Pottery, which was made with blended earthen clays imported from other states. The pottery had fine smooth glazes and classic forms.

Some of first lines, such as the nudes, are very hard to find and command high prices. The value of these early lines is hard to determine because they are not often found for sale. It is known that some of these early pieces of art ware have sold for prices up to $1,500. The prices of all the early 1920s and 1930s art pottery are rapidly increasing due to the age of the pottery and its availability.

The items produced were vases, bowls, compotes, candlesticks, planters, and jardinieres, along with some specialty items. The glazes on the art ware were soft velvety matte, semi-matte, and gloss in an array of colors.

VASE. #631 – 7½", semi-matte white/green, Greek style vase, $48.00 – 62.00.

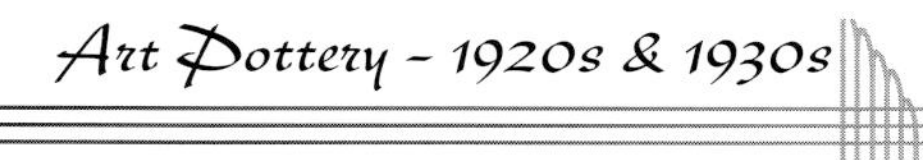

Vase. #447 – 8", gloss coral/tan, Sylvan style vase, $65.00 – 80.00. This vase is designed exactly like its Sylvan Line RumRill counterpart.

Vase. #1165 – 8¾", semi-matte ivory brown wipe, double handled, embossed vase, $55.00 – 65.00. From the collection of Bev & Duane Brown.

Vase. #1245 – 5 ½", semi-matte white/green, round vase, $42.00 – 56.00.

Medallion Line

The following pieces of art ware are from the Medallion line produced in the late 1930s. The line consisted of several groups, among them Magnolia, Vintage, and Renaissance. These groups were produced in a semi-matte finish with a brown wipe of the recesses of the decorations, which were flowers and grapes. The colors known are ivory, turquoise, yellow, and green. Pieces were finished in a color with brown wipe or in ivory with a color wipe.

Some of the flower groups were English Garden, Magnolia, and Cherry Blossom. The grape embossed pieces were the Vintage group. The Medallion line was one of the most popular art pottery lines Red Wing produced. Any of these groups make a wonderful specific line collection.

Vase. #1183 – 6", semi-matte turquoise and brown wipe/white, English Garden vase, $56.00 – 68.00. This color was also used on some of the Magnolia line. It is much harder to find than the ivory and brown wipe. From the collection of Bev & Duane Brown.

Bowl. #1188 – 12", semi-matte turquoise and brown wipe/white, English Garden bowl, $60.00 – 74.00. These English Garden pieces also were made in an ivory and brown wipe, green and brown wipe, and yellow and brown wipe. You will not often see the green, turquoise, and yellow colors. From the collection of Bev & Duane Brown.

Bowl. #621 – 10", semi-matte ivory and brown wipe, Vintage line bowl, $48.00 – 65.00. This bowl was part of the Vintage line. Each piece of art ware in the line was decorated with the grape clusters.

CANDLEHOLDER. #1189 – 5", semi-matte green and brown wipe, English Garden candleholder, $18.00 – 26.00 each. Note the partial wing stamp on the candleholder. Since the wing is partial, it does not add more value to the item. From the collection of Bev & Duane Brown.

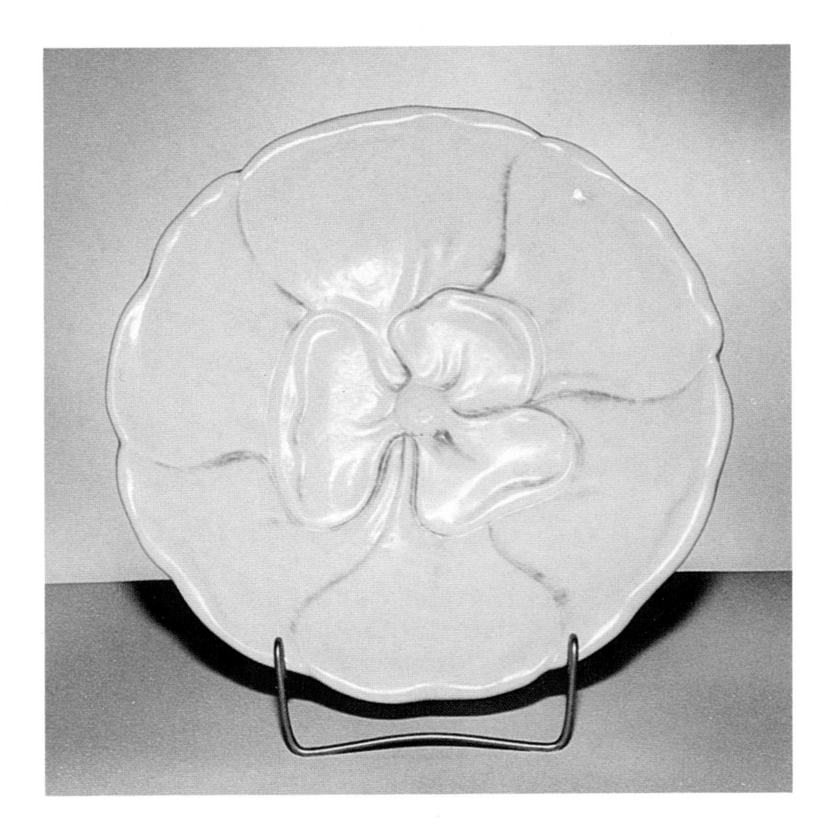

BOWL. #1425 – 12", semi-matte ivory and brown wipe, Magnolia bowl, $52.00 – 70.00.

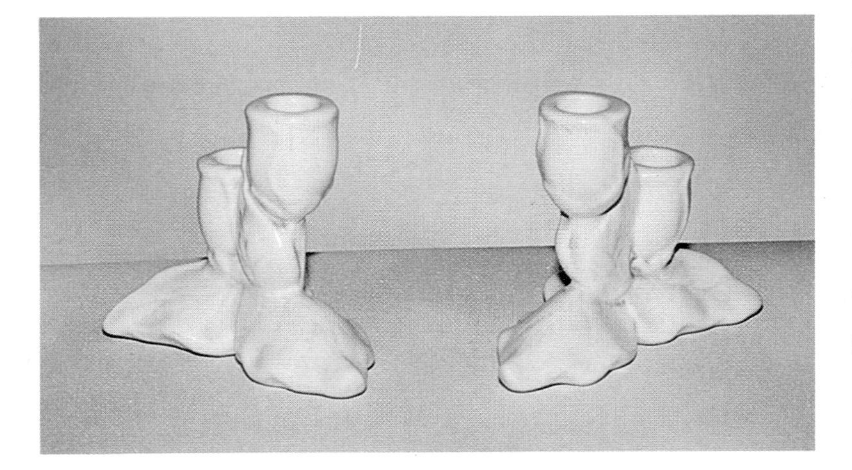

CANDLEHOLDERS. #1228 – 4", semi-matte ivory and brown wipe, Magnolia candleholders, $22.00 – 30.00 each. Some of the Red Wing candleholders you find will not be in pairs. This is especially true with the older vintage ones.

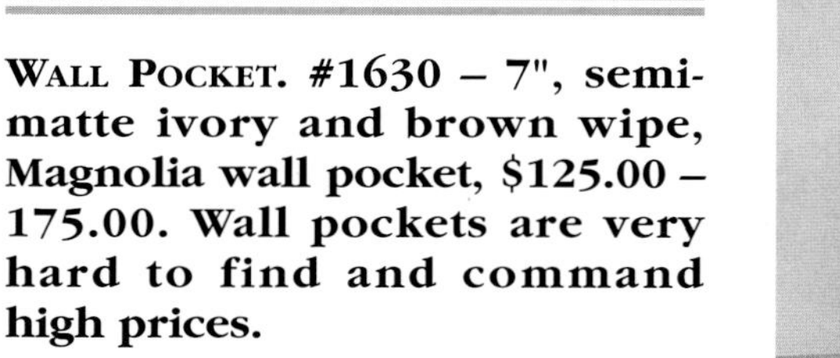

Wall Pocket. #1630 – 7", semi-matte ivory and brown wipe, Magnolia wall pocket, $125.00 – 175.00. Wall pockets are very hard to find and command high prices.

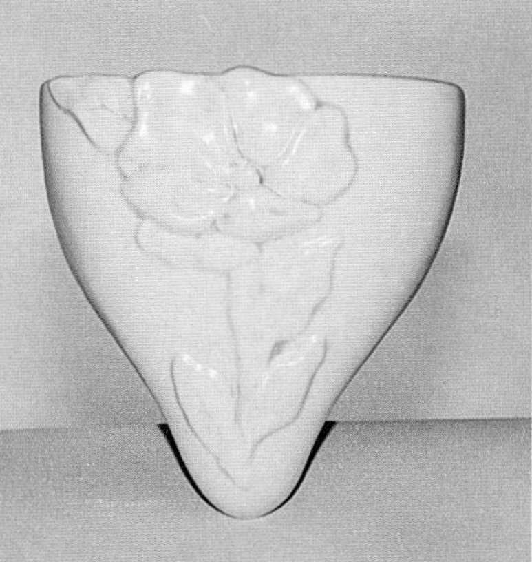

Console Set. Bowl #1425 – 12", Candleholders #1228 – 4", semi-matte ivory and brown wipe, Magnolia console set, $120.00 – 145.00. You will not find many console sets intact, but when you can find them, the pricing is usually a little less than buying the individual pieces.

Console Set. Bowl #621 – 10", Candleholders #622 – 5½", semi-matte ivory and brown wipe, Vintage console set, $98.00 – 120.00.

RumRill Line

The RumRill line was made for George Rumrill who contracted Red Wing to produce his pottery from 1932 – 1937. Dates that the RumRill art ware was produced by Red Wing seem to vary, but these dates seem to be the ones agreed upon most. However, I have seen a Red Wing, RumRill price list dated January 1938; perhaps the RumRill was discontinued late in 1937 or early in 1938.

The pottery was bottom marked RumRill and numbered with the shape number. Quite a few of the RumRill pieces of art ware look identical to some of the Red Wing pottery. This was due to the fact that some of the same molds were used for both. Red Wing also used the same shape number on the bottom of some of the identical RumRill and Red Wing pieces.

RumRill pottery is harder to find than Red Wing due to the short period of time that it was produced at Red Wing and it commands higher prices than its Red Wing counterpart.

George Rumrill continued to produce his pottery at other plants after he left Red Wing. The pieces produced somewhere other than Red Wing are also bottom marked RumRill, although in different styles. Some including a letter preceding the bottom number, others the RumRill was printed in all small letters, and most also had a Made in the USA, or simply USA inscribed along with the name and shape number.

The RumRill produced at Red Wing was bottom marked RumRill along with a shape number. Stickers were also used on some pieces, although they are not found often.

The pottery was produced in many styles of vases, bowls, and candleholders, along with specialty items. These were done in many different matte, semi-matte, and gloss finishes. A list of some of these finishes is in the back of the book, along with a picture of the bottom marking used at Red Wing.

This art pottery is very popular today, not only with Red Wing collectors, but also with RumRill collectors. A collection of RumRill would not only be beautiful, but would provide a great deal of enjoyable searching.

Like Red Wing art ware, RumRill art pottery was produced in a number of different groups, each having their own theme. Among these groups were Grecian, Shell, Sylvan, Indian, Neo-Classic, and Renaissance; examples of these groups follow. There were also many miscellaneous items, but these early groups are not easy to find.

Renaissance Group

The Renaissance group consisted of various vases, bowls, and a candlestick. All were decorated in the same leaf style, and produced in several finish colors. There was also a 12" bowl with a deer-flower-frog insert, which was 10" high. This has become known as the Red Wing Stag.

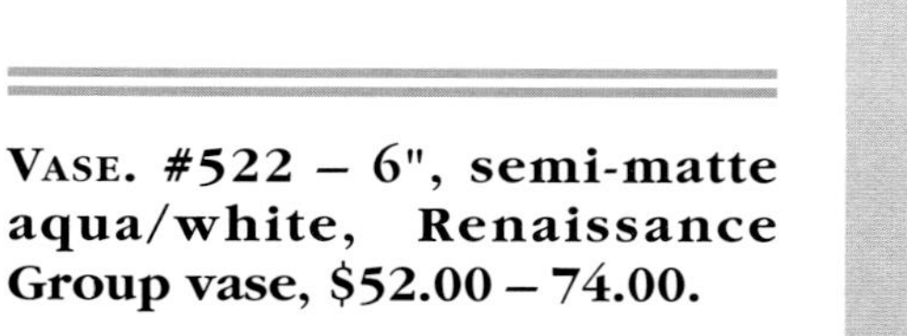

Vase. #522 – 6", semi-matte aqua/white, Renaissance Group vase, $52.00 – 74.00.

Bowl. #530 – 10½", semi-matte ivory/brown wipe, Renaissance Group bowl, $62.00 – 78.00. This color finish was very popular with both Red Wing and RumRill art ware.

Candleholder. **#529 – 6", semi-matte creme/dark brown, Renaissance candleholder, $28.00 – 36.00 each. This candleholder has an unusual sticker on the bottom (see details below).**

Candleholder Bottom Sticker. **Although torn, the sticker states that this is shape #529 and finish #46. Probably used at the factory to enable the workers to select the right shape and finish for an order. These may have been placed on all items and removed after shipment.**

Sylvan Group

The Sylvan group consisted of various style vases, bowls, two different candleholders, and a basket bowl. All were decorated in the same turned-out leaf style and done in a variety of finish colors.

Vase. #445 – 8", gloss coral/tan, Sylvan Group vase, $62.00 – 78.00. This color seems to be one that you might be able to find. From the collection of Bev & Duane Brown.

Neo-Classic Group

The Neo-Classic Group consisted of various style vases, bowls, and a candleholder, produced in a variety of finish colors. All are decorated with ball handles. This line is very popular among collectors, and quite hard to find. The largest of the art ware pieces, a 15" vase #674, has been known to sell for up to $800.00.

Vase. #668 – 10", semi-matte ivory/green, Neo-Classic vase, $175.00 – 225.00. You will find the ball handles were on each piece of the Neo-Classic Group, five or six balls in graduated sizes .

Indian Group

The Indian group consisted of vases, bowls, and a candleholder. There was also a pitcher with a matching stopper. Produced in various finish colors, the art ware had smooth lines with no decoration. Some of the pieces are known to have been finished with the famous Nokomis glaze. This was a semi-matte glaze in various shades of tan and olive, highlighted with copper. The Nokomis is very rare and commands very high prices.

Vase. #291 – 5½", semi-matte ocean green, Indian Group vase, $55.00 – 72.00.

Bowl. #315 – 4½", semi-matte rose/aqua, Indian Group bowl, $68.00 – 76.00.

Grecian Group

The Grecian group consisted mostly of vases. There was a bowl with the same handles as the vase at right. This group was produced in smooth lines, some with circular handles and others with the same handles shown here. Finished in a variety of colors, there is also one shape in this group known to have been produced in the Nokomis finish.

Vase. #506 – 7½", semi-matte orange blend/tan, Grecian Group vase, $68.00 – 75.00.

Classic Group

The Classic group consisted of vases, including a covered vase, bowls, candleholders, and also double and triple candelabras. Like the other RumRill groups, Classic was produced in a variety of finishes. The finishes were changed in each price list with not all of them available at the same time.

Vase. #500 – 5½", semi-matte blue/white stippled, Classic Group vase, $75.00 – 90.00. This finish color was known as Dutch Blue on the RumRill price lists. It was finish #7 on the lists. Notice the white spots on the blue; this was called stippled. This color is quite popular, today known as Dutch blue or stipple.

Shell Group

The Shell group was very ornate, consisting of vases, bowls, candelabra for three candles, and a handled dish made of three flat shells. All the pieces were produced in a shell motif.

Vase. #432 – 7¾", semi-matte ivory/pink, Shell Group vase, $68.00 – 82.00. Notice the intricate shell detail on this vase. All the pieces in this line were produced in elaborate detail.

Miscellaneous Group

Each of the Red Wing catalogs had groups of art ware they labeled miscellaneous. The same was done with the RumRill line. These pieces were just as lovely as some of the named lines as the following examples show.

Vase. #644 – 7", semi-matte ivory/matte blue, miscellaneous swirl vase, $62.00 – 74.00. This finish was #52 on the Rum-Rill Art Pottery price list dated January 1938. Named Rivera it was described as ivory, semi-matte, matte blue lined. Quite a striking finish.

Vase. #641 – 7", matte aqua/gloss white, miscellaneous Greek style vase, $62.00 – 78.00.

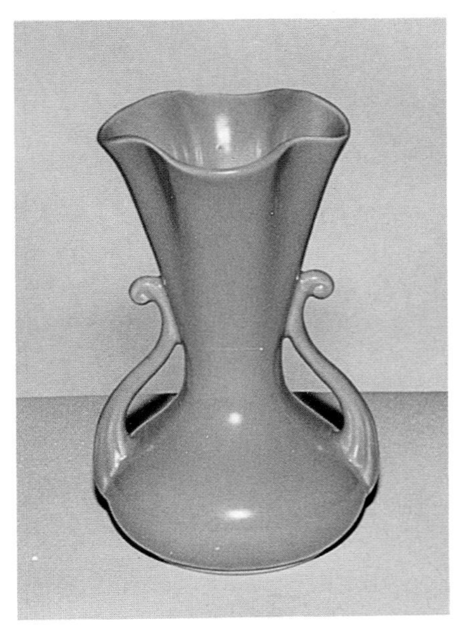

Vase. #505 – 7½", semi-matte blue, miscellaneous vase, $52.00 – 67.00. Almost a baby blue color, this vase is very attractive. This shape number was carried throughout the production of Red Wing. This vase would be ideal for a collection of one shape in multiple colors.

Vase. #636 – 6½", semi-matte turquoise/gloss white, Egyptian style miscellaneous vase, $62.00 – 78.00.

Bowl. #341 – 7", semi-matte ivory/matte blue, miscellaneous bowl, $68.00 – 76.00. This is also #52 Rivera finish.

Art Pottery – 1940s

During the 1940s era, Red Wing Art Pottery continued to be produced in a wide array of colors and adorned with decorations, although not quite as ornate as some of the early pottery. They also included considerable miscellaneous items and fewer line names.

Some of the early lines such as Magnolia and Renaissance were carried into the 1940s production. This practice of adding some of the prior year's shapes to the new items continued through the 1950s and 1960s. Some of the pottery shapes carried through all the years of production, produced in a different finish in each era.

The art pottery in this chapter is from the author's collection, unless otherwise noted.

Vases

VASE. #1160 – 9½", gloss luster blue/coral, leaf motif vase, $58.00 – 72.00. This would be a good choice for those who want to arrange their collection by color. There were numerous pieces produced with this finish, many of them very decorative. It is quite pretty. Other art ware this color follows.

VASE. #1174 – 7", semi-matte pink/white, leaf embossed vase, $48.00 – 62.00.

VASE. #884 – 10", semi-matte white, footed vase, $48.00 – 65.00. Simple but elegant, this vase would look good in any setting.

VASE. #110 – 7½", semi-matte burnt orange/gray, rose decorated vase, $58.00 – 72.00. The dark spots you see on this vase are gold blotches in the finish. This is quite unusual and will not be seen often. From the collection of Bev & Duane Brown.

VASE. #1151 – 8", semi-matte white/green, Egyptian symbol embossed vase, $70.00 – 90.00. This vase with the Egyptian symbols seems to be more expensive than some of the other vases of this era. This color finish is fairly common in Red Wing Art Pottery.

VASE. #1115 – 7¼", semi-matte green/white, leaf embossed vase, $52.00 – 68.00.

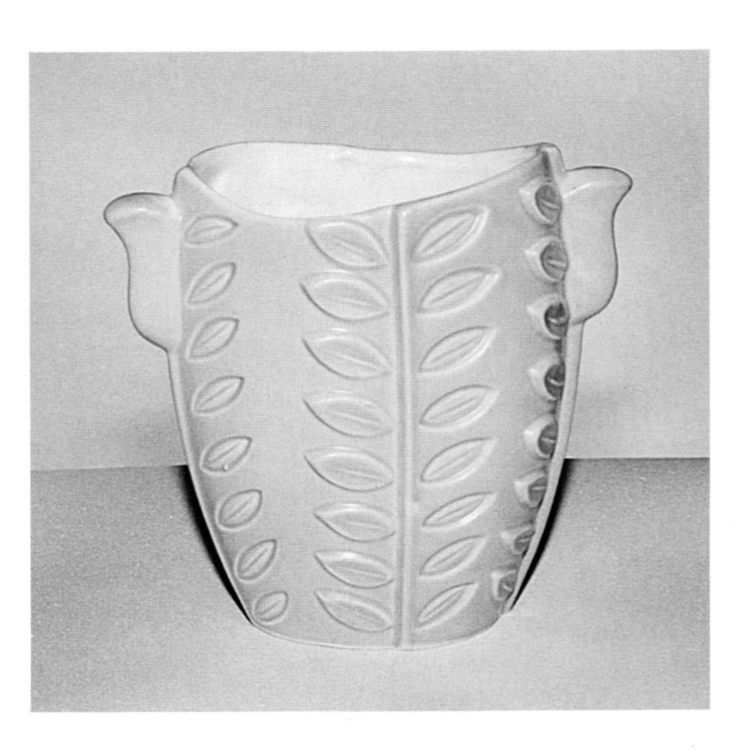

VASE. #1162 – 9", gloss gray/yellow, decorator purple leaf trimmed vase, $68.00 – 75.00. The decorator pieces have contrasting colors on the trim. This shape was also produced in plain colors. The decorator vases would be an excellent selection for a color collection. They were produced in a wide variety of shapes and colors. From the collection of Bev & Duane Brown.

VASE. #1103 – 8¼", gloss tan/green, decorator brown leaf trimmed vase, $48.00 – 62.00. From the collection of Bev & Duane Brown.

Vase. #1377 – 10", semi-matte aqua/white, oil lamp style vase, $75.00 – 95.00. From the collection of Bev & Duane Brown.

Vase. #1377 – 10", semi-matte maroon/gray, oil lamp style vase, $85.00 – 110.00. This maroon color finish in any piece of art ware commands higher prices. From the collection of Bev & Duane Brown.

VASE. #926 – 7½", semi-matte Dutch blue/white stipple, red wing label, $95.00 – 110.00. This finish known as Dutch blue or stipple also commands higher prices; the wing label also adds to the pricing. This color finish, although hard to find, would make a beautiful color collection.

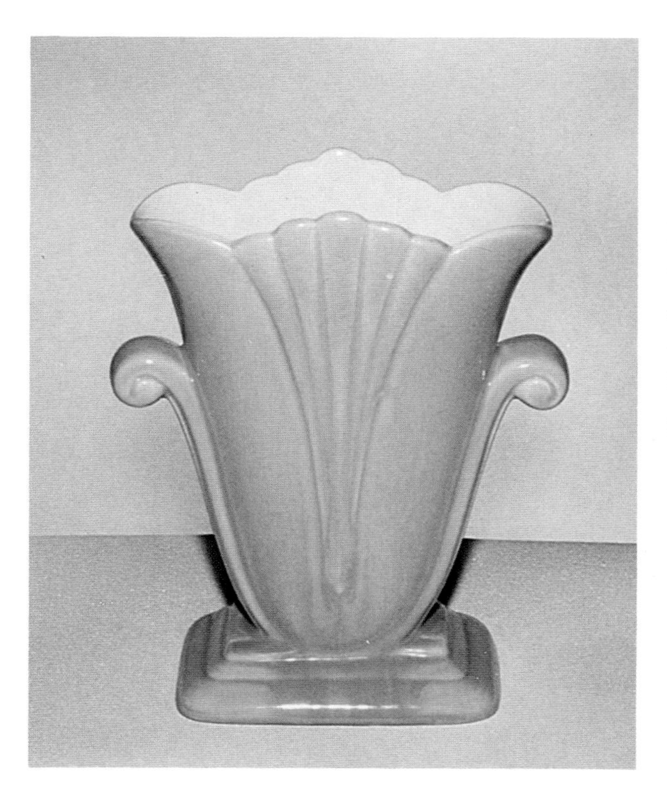

VASE. #886 – 7½", semi-matte orange/tan, tulip shaped vase, $42.00 – 56.00. This vase also was produced in identical shape #885 in 9½" size.

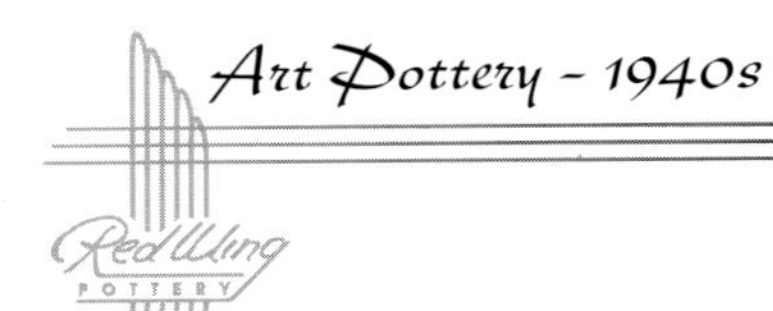

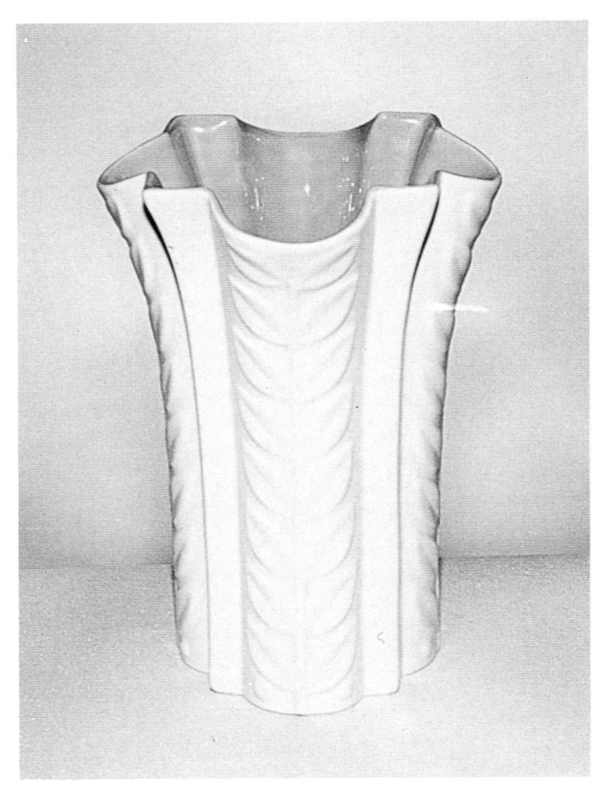

VASE. #1155 – 10", semi-matte white/green, leaf embossed vase, $48.00 – 60.00.

VASE. #1111 – 7½", semi-matte pink/white, double handled vase, $54.00 – 62.00.

Vase. #1204 – 10", gloss yellow/gray, brown leaf trimmed vase, $48.00 – 65.00. From the collection of Bev & Duane Brown.

Vase. #1105 – 8", gloss luster blue/coral, gold wing label, purple leaf decorator vase, $72.00 – 84.00. One of the many pieces in the luster blue/coral finish, its intact wing label increases the value.

Vase. #1107 – 7", gloss gray/yellow, purple flower trimmed decorator vase, $58.00 – 70.00. From the collection of Bev & Duane Brown.

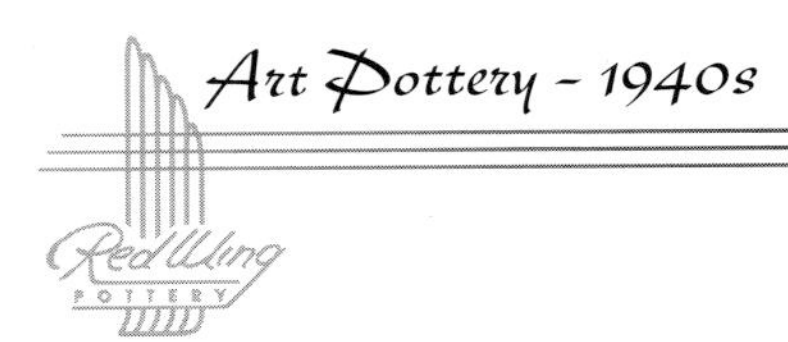

VASE. #1120 – 7½", gloss light orchid/yellow, purple leaf trimmed deer motif decorator vase, $54.00 – 72.00. The art ware shown in this section with different color trim appears to be part of the Decoration Line. These shapes were also produced in plain color finishes. Prices will be higher for the multi-colored pieces.

VASE. #1102 – 8", gloss luster blue/coral, purple leaf trimmed decorator vase, $62.00 – 75.00. From the collection of Bev & Duane Brown.

Vase. #1159 – 8", semi-matte pink/white, embossed vase, $72.00 – 86.00. You will find that this pink and white finish is higher priced, perhaps because it is harder to find. The embossed finish also adds value. From the collection of Bev & Duane Brown.

Vase. #889 – 8", semi-matte white/green, flower embossed vase, $56.00 – 68.00. This finish is another good one to collect if you are going to organize by color. You will find a good selection in this color; the luster blue and coral is harder to find.

VASE. #1053 – 8", semi-matte green/ white, trophy style vase, $42.00 – 55.00.

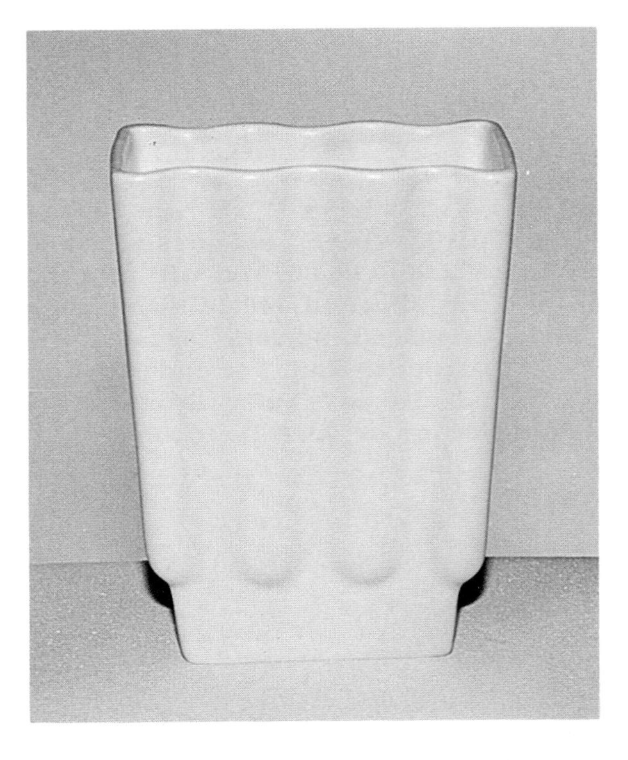

VASE. #1237 – 8", semi-matte pink/white, footed vase, $48.00 – 56.00.

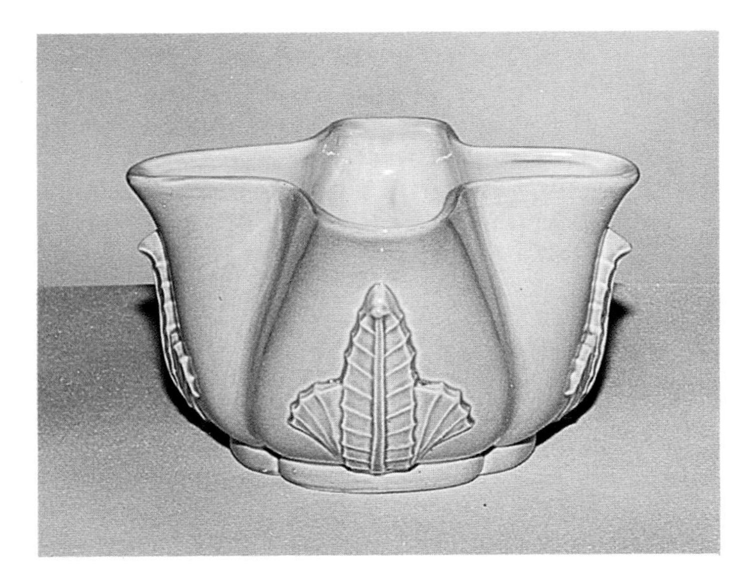

VASE. #1241 – 5", gloss luster blue/coral, leaf embossed vase, $52.00 – 68.00. You will notice that the luster blue and coral finish tends to vary in color. This is because the colors were mixed by hand and would change slightly with each production run. You will find this is also true with the white and green finish. From the collection of Bev & Duane Brown.

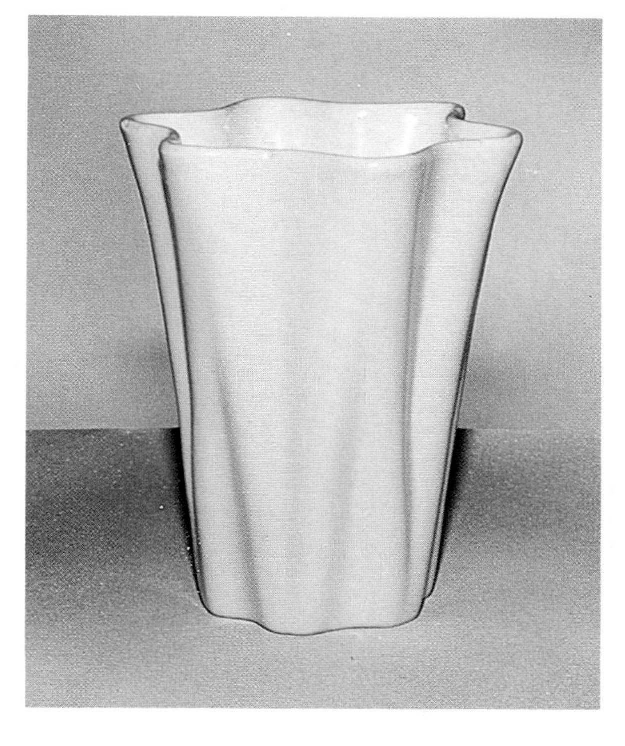

VASE. #887 – 7½", semi-matte pink/white, flared top vase, $56.00 – 67.00. From the collection of Bev & Duane Brown.

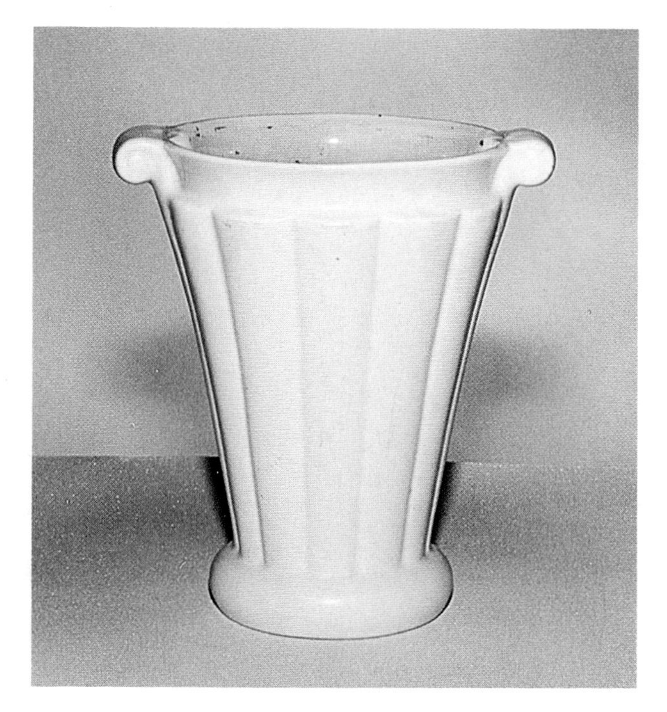

VASE. #880 – 8", semi-matte white/green, tapered vase, $48.00 – 56.00. From the collection of Bev & Duane Brown.

VASE. #1107 – 7¼", matte green/white, leaf embossed vase, $56.00 – 68.00.

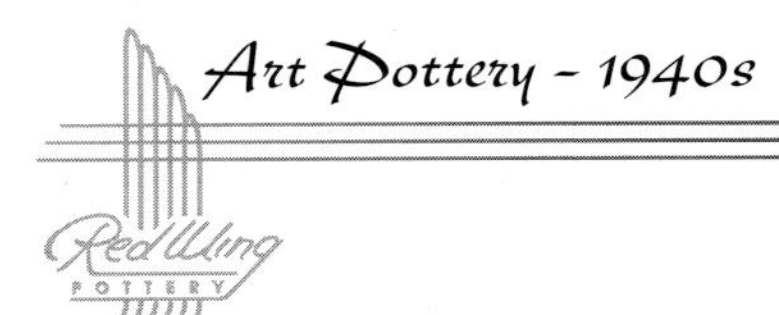

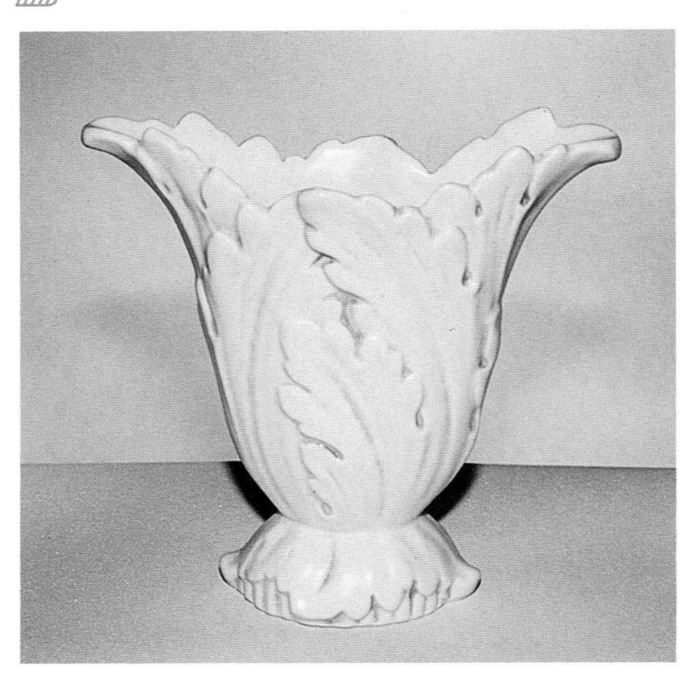

Vase. #1096 – 9", semi-matte white/brown wipe, leaf motif vase, $72.00 – 84.00. The brown wipe finish commands higher prices because it is quite hard to find. This finish was produced by applying a brown stain to the piece and then wiping off the excess, leaving the brown in the recessed parts of the trim. This created a lovely piece of art ware. Some art ware was produced with a green wipe; these green wipe pieces are quite rare and hardly ever found.

Vase. #929 – 10", semi-matte white/brown wipe, leaf trimmed vase, $62.00 – 78.00.

Vase. #1240 – 5", semi-matte pink/white, cornucopia type vase, $48.00 – 56.00.

VASE. #952 – 6", gloss blue, swirl vase, $48.00 – 60.00. Although simple, this is a very lovely vase.

VASE. #1056 – 9½", semi-matte white/green, urn type vase, shown here with the lid. $84.00 – 98.00.

VASE. #1056 – 9½", semi-matte white/green, gold wing label, urn type vase, $84.00 – 98.00 with lid. Shown here with the lid off so that the inside color is visible; vases with lids are not often found. A pair of these vases, with bowl #1055 – 12½", is shown in the 1940s Red Wing catalogs as a console set. The bowl has the same handles as the vase. The vase with the lid on is shown above.

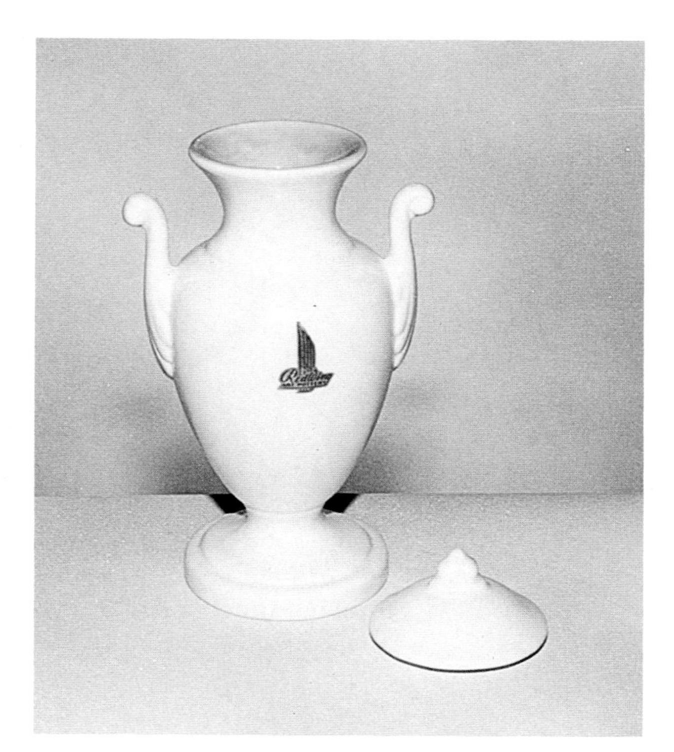

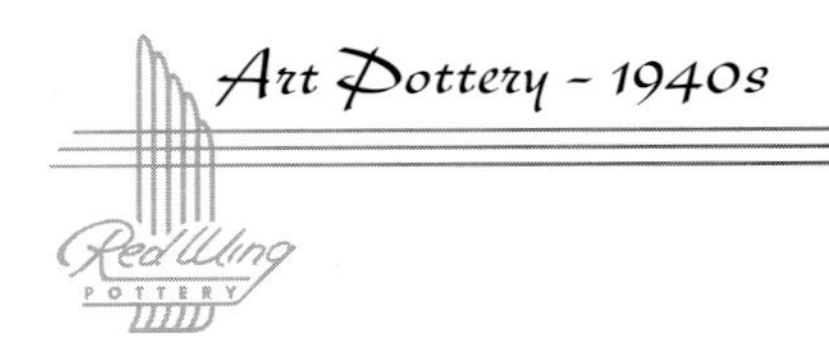

Bowls

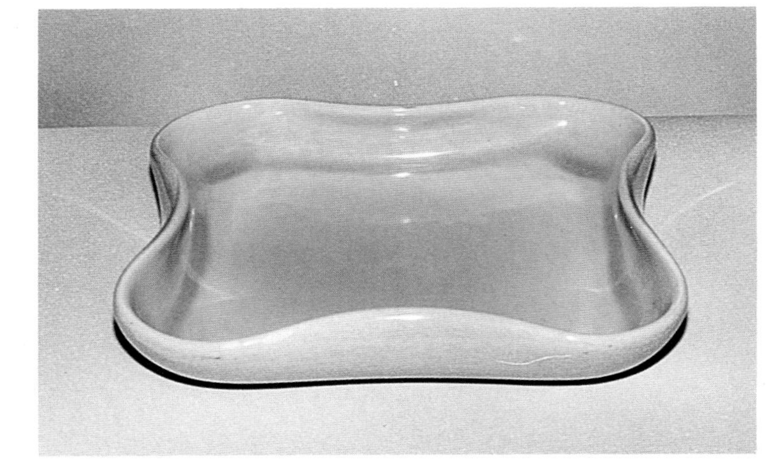

Bowl. #1037 – 8", gloss luster blue/coral, square bowl, $38.00 – 46.00. You will not find many bowls of this vintage. Later in the 1950s and 1960s many types of bowl were produced and are readily found.

Bowl. #276 – 6", semi-matte white/mustard marble, classic style bowl, $42.00 – 56.00. Notice the unusual marble finish inside this bowl.

Candleholders

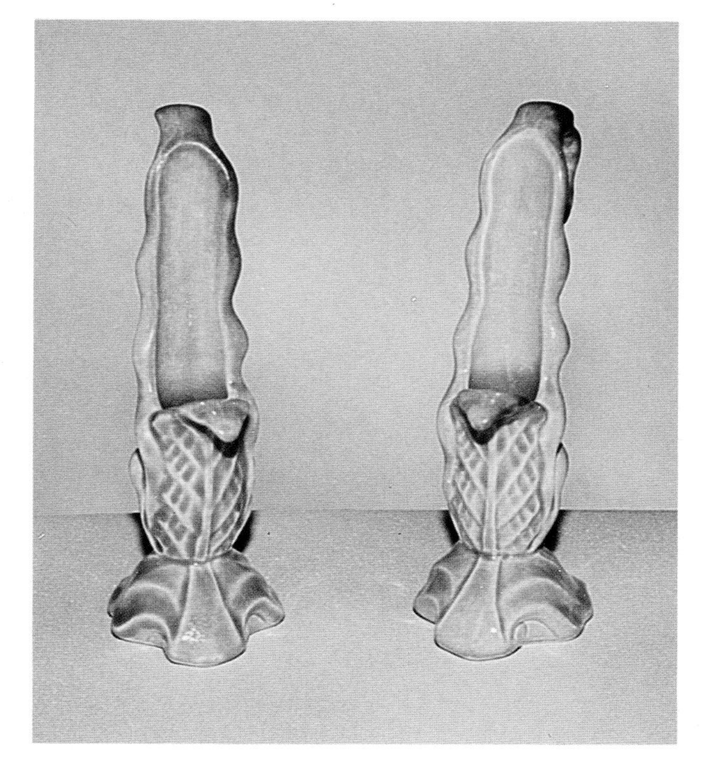

CANDLEHOLDERS. #1286 – 8", gloss turquoise, leaf motif pair of candleholders, $30.00 – 38.00 each. Called candlesticks in the Red Wing catalogs, they were not many different styles produced in any vintage. Candleholders of any style are harder to find than other art ware.

Centerpiece

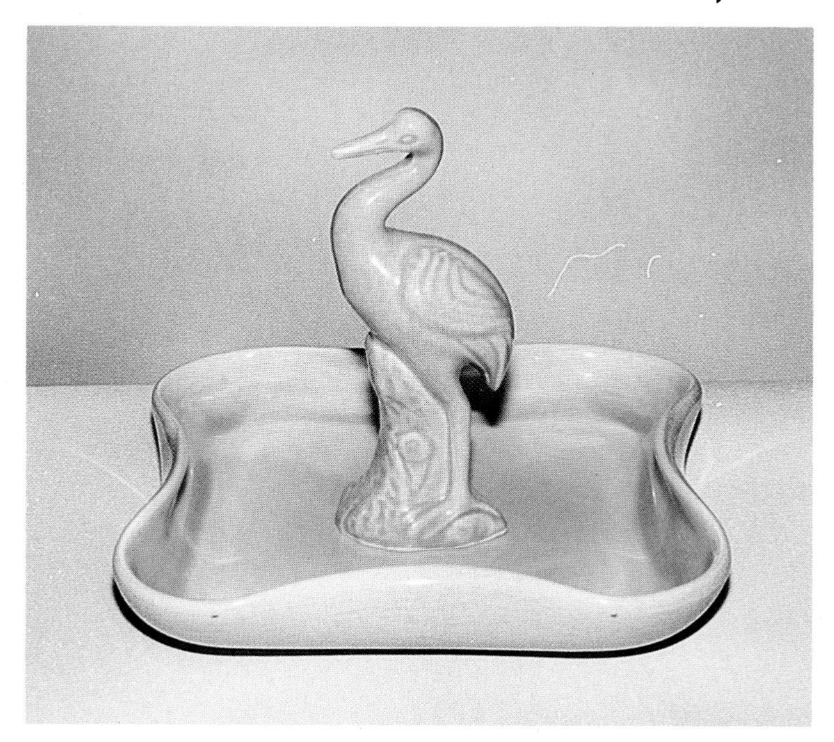

CENTERPIECE. #1037 – 8" bowl, unmarked bird figurine – 5", gloss luster blue/coral centerpiece set, $60.00 – 72.00.

Wall Pockets

Wall pockets make a beautiful and unique collection. They are quite hard to find, but worth the search. You will also find them to be more expensive than some of the other art ware, because they are quite scarce. This would also be a good collection for someone with limited space, since the collection could be hung on walls, and flowers can be added to match your décor.

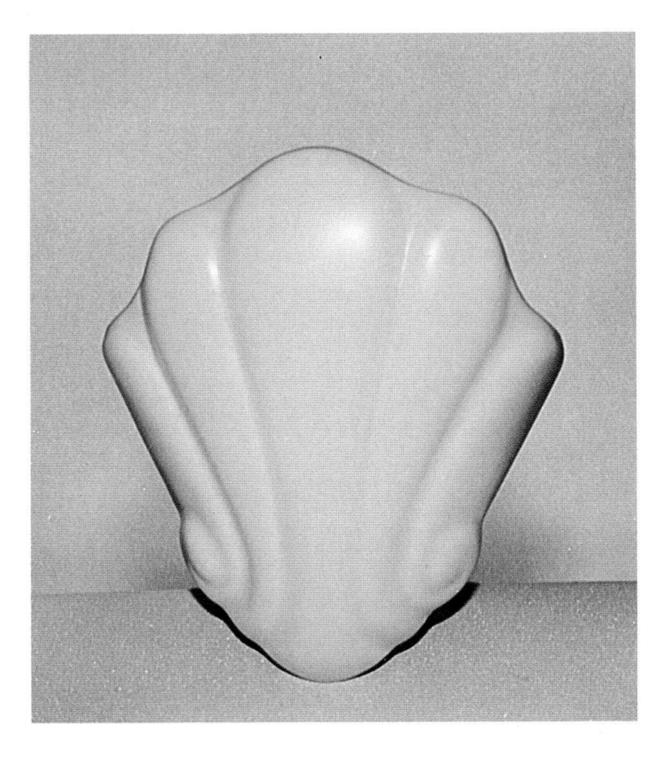

WALL POCKET. #1254 – 7", semi-matte pink/white, sconce type wall pocket, $72.00 – 95.00. Wall pockets of any kind are very hard to find.

Planters

Planters also make a very nice collection, and there were many varieties of small planters produced by Red Wing. Among these were animal planters such as bears, ducks, donkeys, deer, and rabbit. Produced in a variety of colors with sizes starting at 4", they make a very pretty collection. They are, however, quite hard to find and the pricing can be high.

PLANTER. No bottom mark – 6½", matte blue, silver wing label, lamb planter, $110.00 – 145.00. Shown in a 1948 Red Wing catalog, this planter is known to have also been produced in matte gray, yellow, white, and green. Red Wing produced a number of planters in different animal shapes. Any of these planters is quite rare and not often found for sale.

Figurine

FIGURINE. 5", gloss coral/blue, bird figurine, $38.00 – 46.00. Part of the centerpiece shown on page 55. Although unmarked, this figurine is advertised as Red Wing. There is also a larger size.

Art Pottery - 1950s

As Red Wing entered the 1950s and 1960s production era, they introduced a wide array of colors, along with a contemporary look in a lot of the art ware. They branched out from the traditional colors and shapes they used in the 1930s and 1940s.

Like in previous years, some of the 1930s and 1940s art ware shapes were carried into the new production period. In the mid 1950s Red Wing introduced a variety of new art pottery, all done in a gloss glaze, most with the Art Deco look. The colors ranged from the traditional white to orchid, produced in a wide variety of odd-shaped pieces. Some of the art pottery of this period is not as easily recognized by sight as the earlier art ware. Once you become familiar with some of the new colors and shapes, identification will be easier.

Continuing the trend started in the 1940s, the 1950s art pottery did not use a lot of line names. They were grouped in the Red Wing catalogs by items, such as vases, bowls, compotes, and planters, along with a miscellaneous section. The candleholders, which were called candlesticks in the earlier catalogs, were usually grouped on a page with a matching console bowl, and were sold as a console set. They also introduced many varieties of ashtrays, a cake salver, and large contemporary cornucopias.

Along with these items, they continued to produce novelty planters, and introduced some unique music motif planters. There were a banjo, violin, and a piano, all produced in detail to resemble the real musical instruments. The violins are found more often than the others, and are still affordable. A piano planter found in excellent condition can command up to $500 depending on the color. There is also a cart planter with movable brass wheels.

The colors of the art pottery line were broadened to include a wide array of bright glossy finishes. They also continued the plain two-tone finishes. Introduced in the mid 1950s was a line of fleck colors. The color was flecked with a light black or brown and was used on solid fleck art ware as well as two-tone. On the two-tone, the fleck color was usually used on the outside with a solid color finish on the inside.

There are several of these fleck colors, fleck yellow, fleck green, fleck zephyr pink, fleck Nile blue, and fleck orchid. The art ware done in these colors was quite attractive and modern looking. Although harder to find, these finishes would be a good choice for a collection organized by color. You will find the blue and pink fleck most often.

The look and colors of the art ware during this period was changing with the times as the following photographs show.

The art pottery in this chapter is from the author's collection unless otherwise noted.

Vases

VASE. #M3007 – 12", semi-matte burnt orange, jug type vase, $58.00 – 70.00. This shape number is shown as part of the Decorator Line done in crystalline glazes in the Red Wing catalog for fall 1959. However, the number is not preceded with the M, which is the designer's, Charles Murphy, initial. Therefore, it is not certain that it was part of that line; the pricing would be a lot higher if that could be confirmed. A vase from the Decorator Line with a silver green finish has been known to sell for several hundred dollars. From the collection of Bev & Duane Brown.

VASE. #505 – 7½", gloss fleck orchid/semi-matte orchid, fluted top vase, $42.00 – 58.00. This shape number is one that was produced from the 1930s through the 1960s. You will find a variety of different colors on this piece of art ware. This piece would make a good choice if you wanted a collection with one item in a wide array of colors.

VASE. #1590 – 10", gloss yellow, swirl vase, $48.00 – 56.00. From the collection of Bev & Duane Brown.

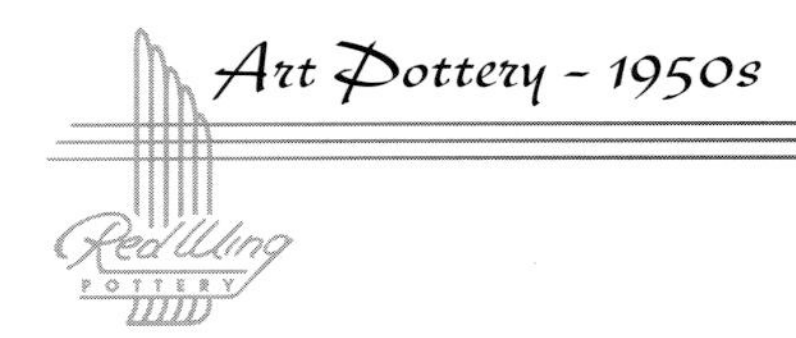

VASE. M1439 – 6", semi-matte white/ green, leaf footed vase, $42.00 – 54.00.

VASE. #871 – 7½", gloss maroon/gray, trophy style vase, $46.00 – 58.00.

VASE. #1120 – 9", semi-matte cypress green, compote vase, $38.00 – 52.00. This vase was also produced in the 1960s and placed in the Floraline section in 1960s catalogs.

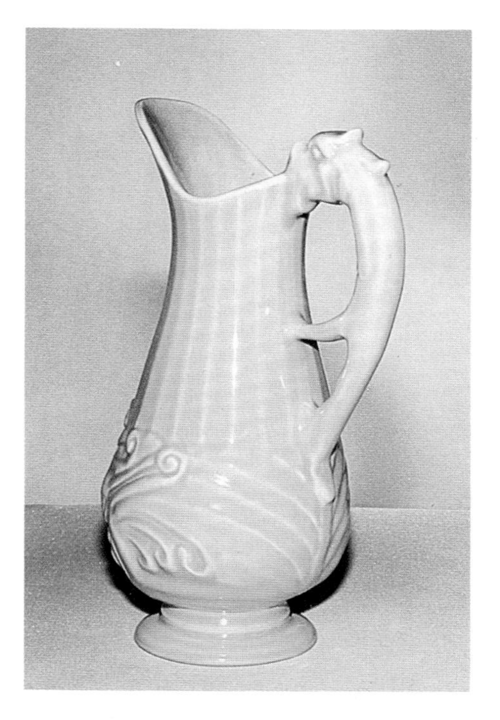

VASE. #220 – 10", gloss yellow/gray, fish handled pitcher vase, $90.00 – 120.00. This vase was also produced in the 1940s, with different finish colors. A maroon vase in this shape number is known to have sold for $375.00. You will not often find these vases, and the price will be determined by the vintage and finish color. From the collection of Bev & Duane Brown.

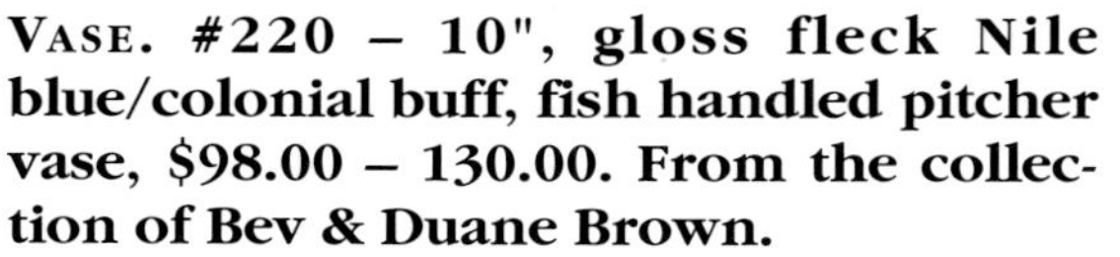

VASE. #220 – 10", gloss fleck Nile blue/colonial buff, fish handled pitcher vase, $98.00 – 130.00. From the collection of Bev & Duane Brown.

VASE. #1196 – 10", gloss gray/yellow, purple flower handled vase, $48.00 – 62.00. This vase has the look of the earlier Decorator Line, perhaps carried over to the 1950s.

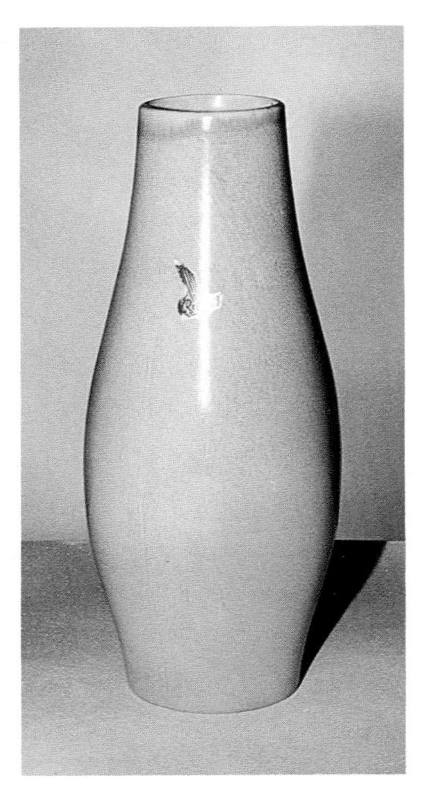

VASE. #686 – 12", gloss buff/light celadon, silver wing label, bulbous cylinder type vase, $48.00 – 56.00. This shape number was used several times by Red Wing. There is a vase with this number in 1930s miscellaneous and also in 1960s Chromoline. They are identical in shape, only the finishes are different. From the collection of Bev & Duane Brown.

VASE. #357 – 8", gloss gray/coral, leaf trimmed footed vase, $38.00 – 46.00. From the collection of Bev & Duane Brown.

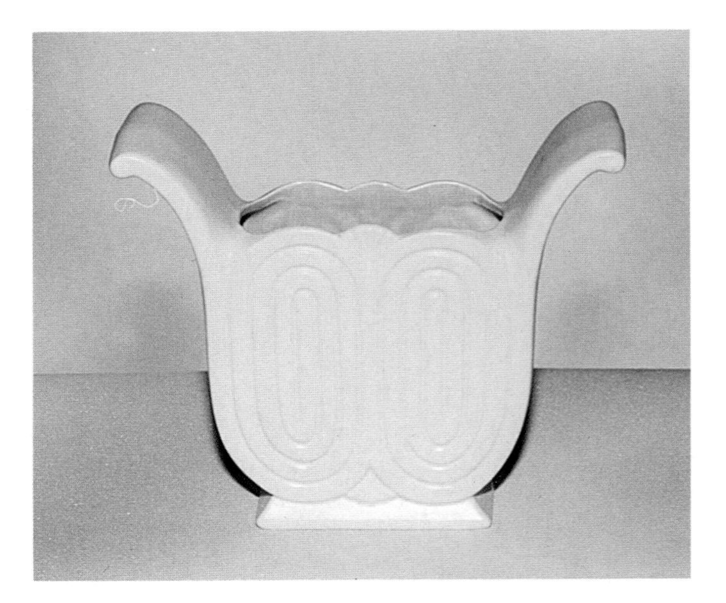

VASE. #1168 – 7", semi-matte white/green, flat handled vase, $42.00 – 56.00.

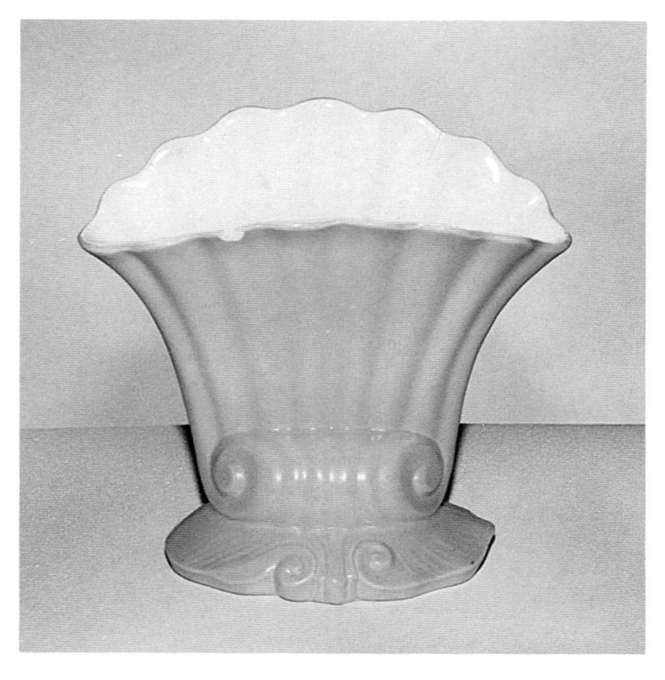

VASE. #1295 – 7", semi-matte orange/white, shell type vase, $36.00 – 48.00.

VASE. #1202 – 5½", gloss blue/coral, contoured vase, $34.00 – 42.00.

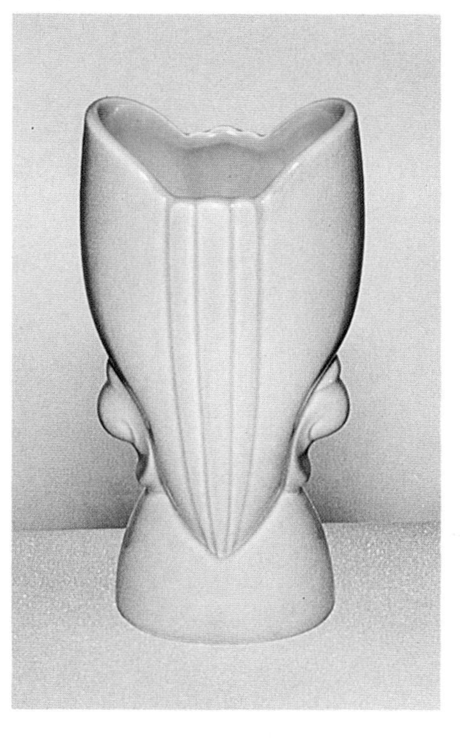

VASE. #B1397 – 7", gloss gray/coral, tapered vase, $32.00 – 40.00.

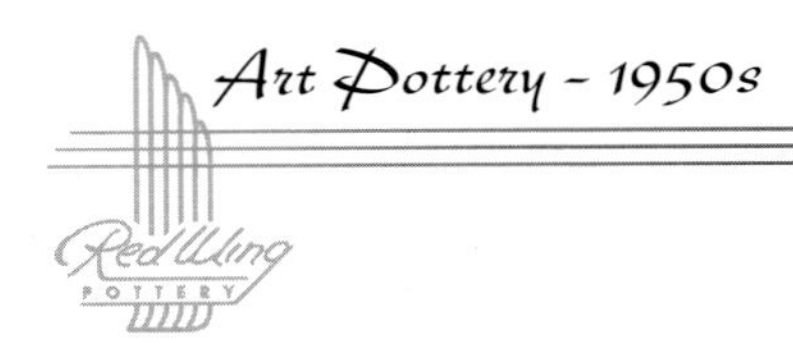

VASE. #M1457 – 7½", gloss fleck yellow, spike trimmed vase, $42.00 – 56.00.

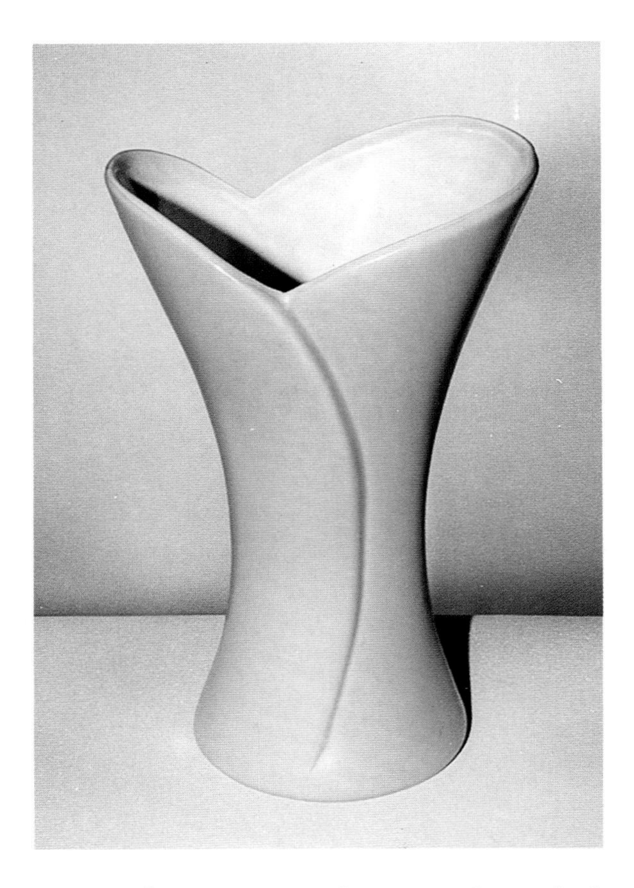

VASE. #1625 – 10", semi-matte salmon/yellow, petal shaped vase $44.00 – 56.00.

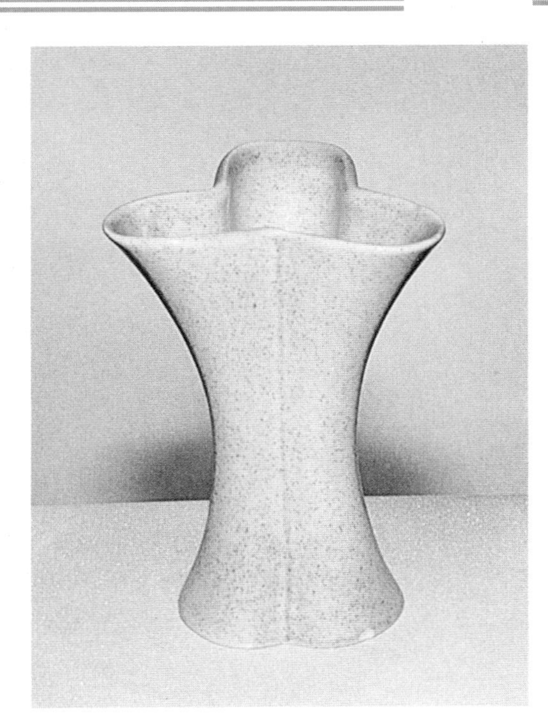

VASE. #1556 – 6", gloss fleck zephyr pink, cloverleaf vase, $38.00 – 44.00.

Bowls

Monarch Line

The Monarch line consisted of two patterns, Gothic and Contemporary. Advertised in the Red Wing catalog as a line of planters and low bowls, there is also one vase in each pattern. Pictured below is the Gothic pattern. The Contemporary pattern is similar in color with a stripe design.

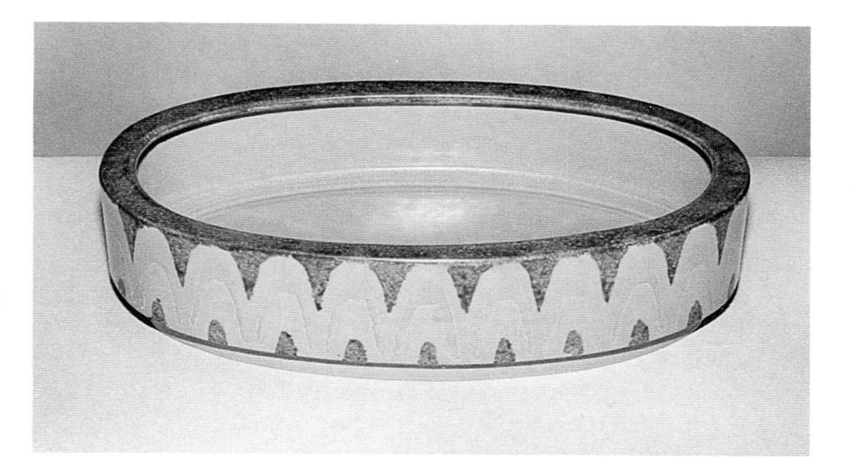

Bowl. #937 – 10", semi-matte green/brown trim, Gothic bowl, $40.00 – 52.00. This bowl is from the Monarch Line.

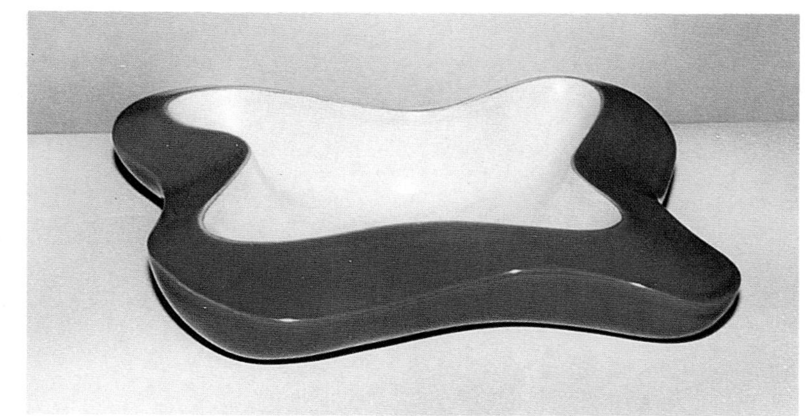

Bowl. #1372 – 11", gloss maroon/ white crackle, contoured bowl, $38.00 – 48.00. Although hard to see, the inside of this bowl has a crackle finish.

Bowl. #414 – 7", gloss brown/orange, flat bowl, $32.00 – 44.00.

Bowl. #M1448 – 8", gloss gray/ yellow, character embossed bowl, $38.00 – 46.00.

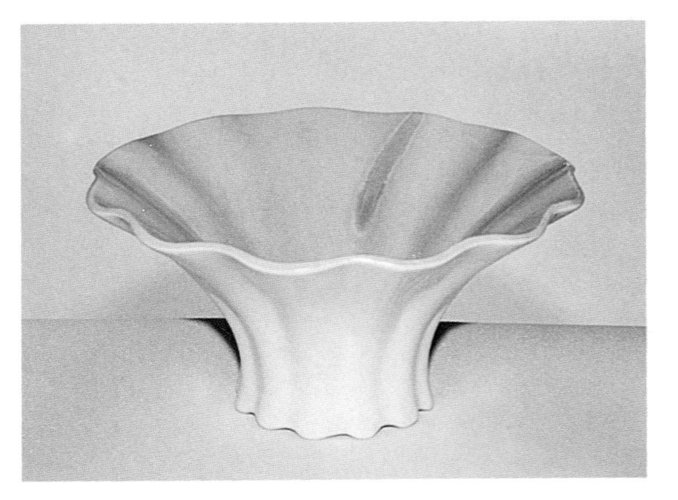

Bowl. #1264 – 9", semi-matte white/ green, large top tapered bowl, $44.00 – 56.00. Notice the brown spot inside this bowl. The brown color was fired with the inside glaze, perhaps a mistake or a blended glaze.

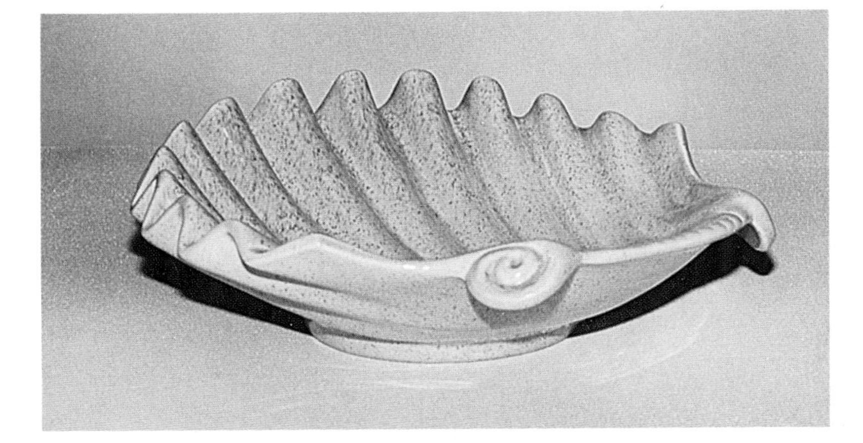

Bowl. #M1567 – 9", gloss fleck Nile blue, shell bowl, $44.00 – 56.00. This another example of the different pieces of art ware in the fleck Nile blue color. From the collection of Bev & Duane Brown.

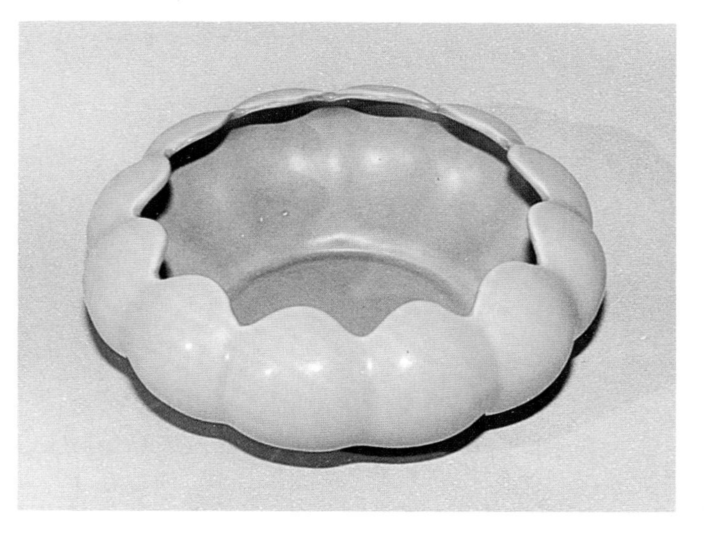

Bowl. #278 – 9", gloss yellow/gray, classic type bowl, $40.00 – 52.00. From the collection of Bev & Duane Brown.

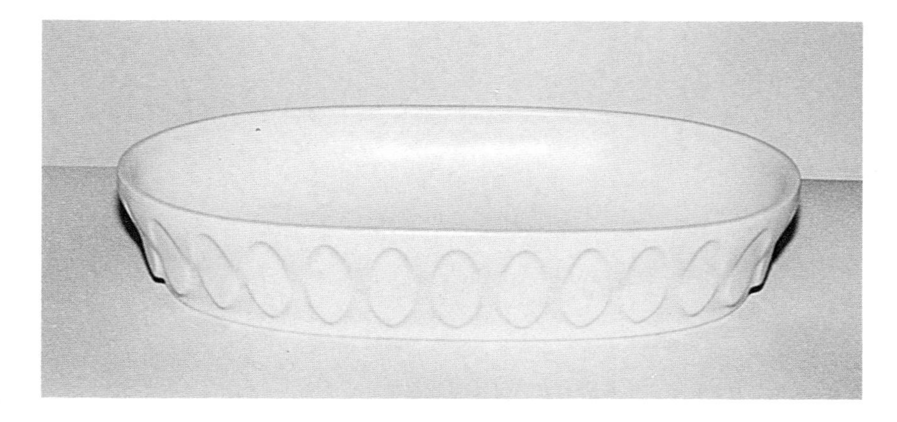

Bowl. ##835 – 8", matte white, low concave bowl, $35.00 – 46.00. This bowl is rounded inside and very shallow.

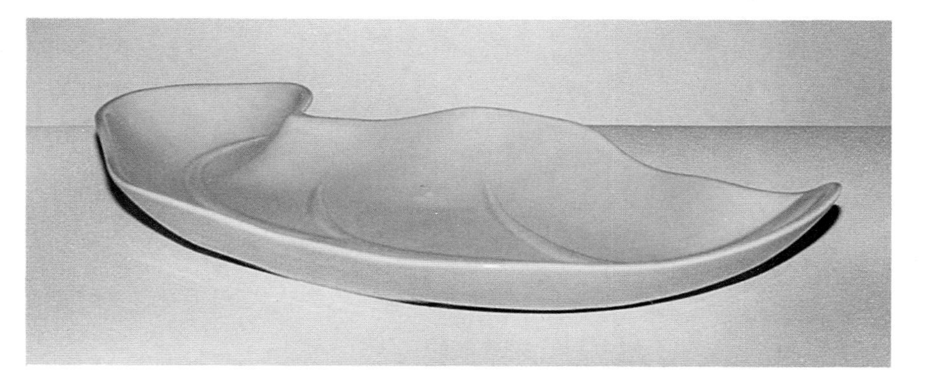

Bowl. #1251 – 12", gloss luster blue/coral, leaf shape bowl, $42.00 – 54.00. This bowl has a detailed vein on the inside and bottom.

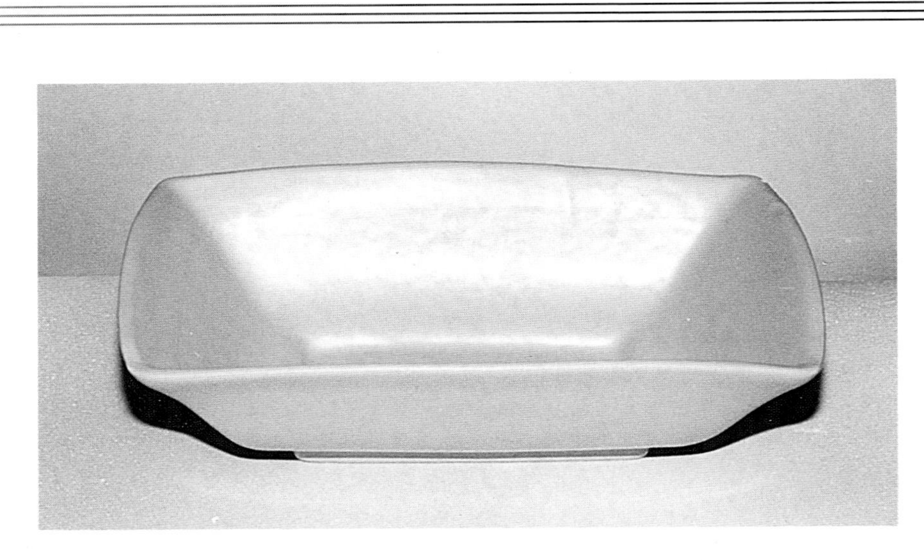

Bowl. #5015 – 9", matte gray, rectangular bowl, $30.00 – 38.00.

Bowl. #M1535 – 4", gloss brown/turquoise, silver wing label, triangular hand-painted bowl, $38.00 – 48.00. The colors on the inside of this bowl were hand painted. The wing label is quite faded and does not add much value to this item.

Bowl. #1382 – 12", gloss gray/coral, boat type bowl, $35.00 – 42.00.

Bowl. #M1537 – 4", gloss brown/ turquoise, round hand painted bowl, $38.00 – 48.00. A counterpart to the bowl on the preceding page, the inside was also hand painted. Notice the lines are different from the first bowl.

Bowl. #1620 – 10", semi-matte salmon, scalloped-edged bowl, $42.00 – 56.00. This bowl was advertised as a console bowl in the Red Wing catalog. There were matching candleholders to form the set.

Bowl. #1483 – 18", fleck zephyr pink, spiked bowl, $48.00 – 60.00. This bowl sold for $6.00 in the fall 1957 Red Wing catalog, one of the higher priced items of that time. From the collection of Bev & Duane Brown.

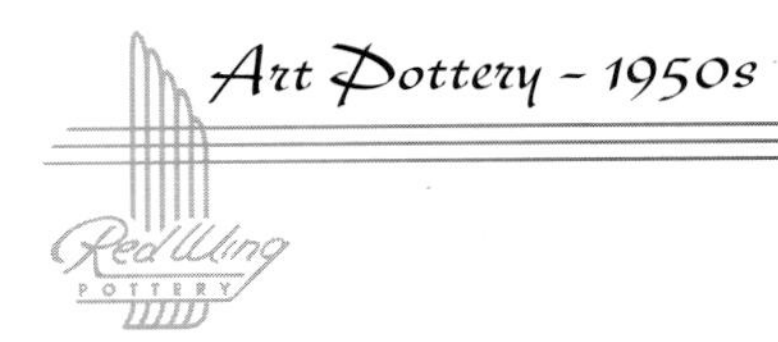

Compotes

Compote. #5022 – 7", fleck Nile blue/colonial buff, gold wing label, modern compote, $48.00 – 60.00.

Decorator Brass Line

Introduced in 1958, this was one of the few line names given in the 1950s era, and was the only line produced by Red Wing to be trimmed in brass. There were several styles of vases, planters, and compotes. Produced in a variety of color finishes including black and the fleck colors, this was very attractive art ware, and tends to be higher in price because of its scarcity.

Compote. #M1598 – 8", semi-matte white, medium pedestal brass handled compote, $48.00 – 60.00.

Candleholders

CANDLEHOLDERS. #1619 – 4½", semi-matte salmon, scalloped-edged candleholders, $32.00 – 40.00 pair. Sold as a pair, these candleholders were part of a console set with bowl #1620.

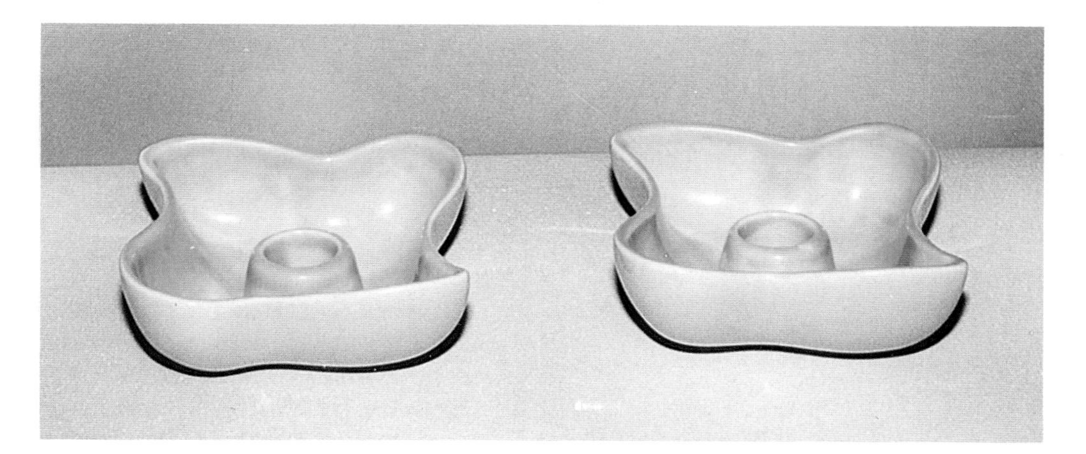

CANDLEHOLDERS. #B1411 – 4", gloss gray/coral, petal shaped candleholders, $26.00 – 38.00 pair.

Console Sets

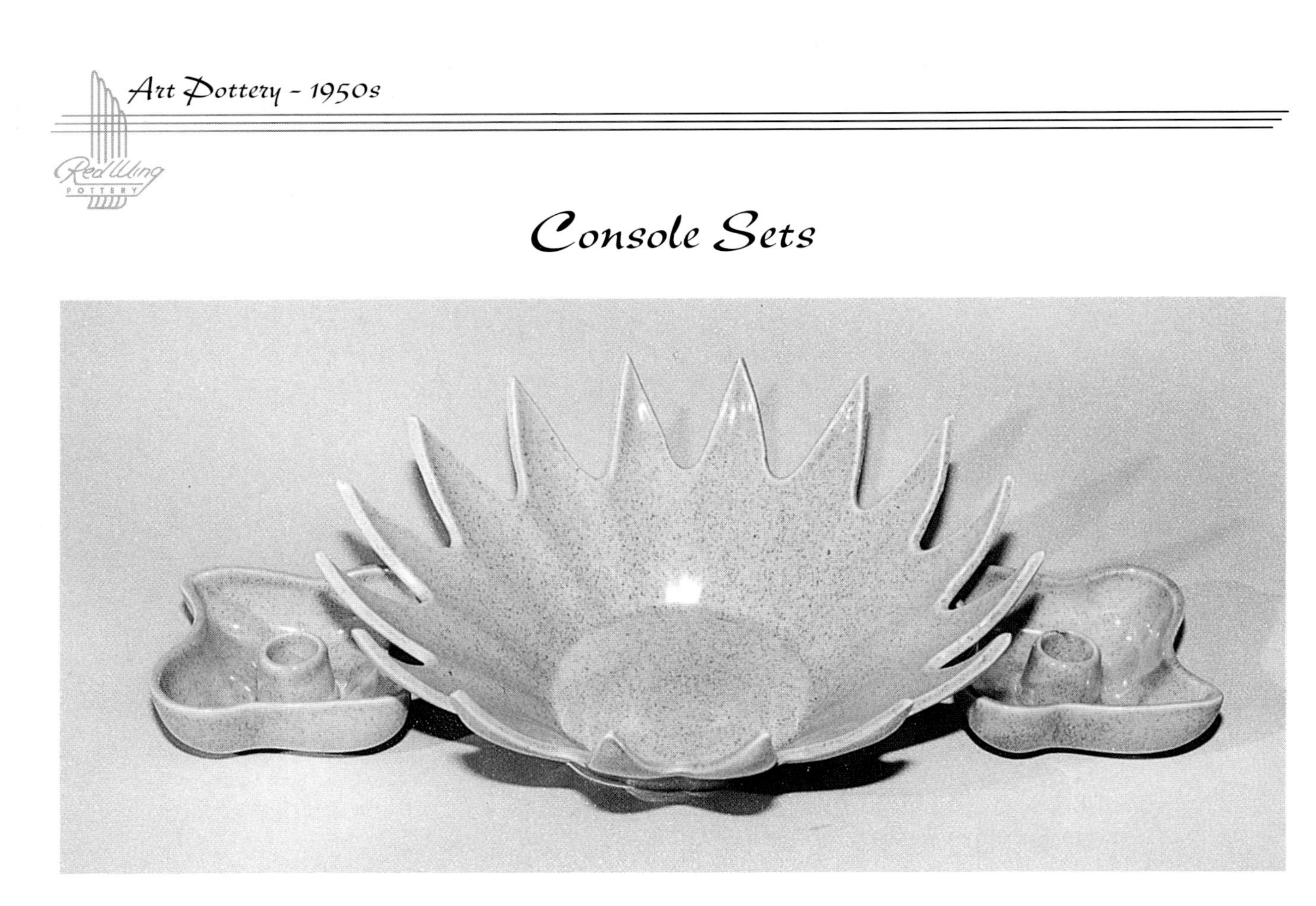

CONSOLE SET. Bowl #M1483 – 18", Candleholders #B1411 – 4", fleck zephyr pink console set, $72.00 – 98.00. Candleholders sold separately $32.00 – 40.00 pair. There is also a pair of spike trimmed candleholders that go with this bowl. From the collection of Bev & Duane Brown.

CONSOLE SET. Bowl #278 – 9", Figurine #1308 – 10", gloss yellow/gray classic type console set $145.00 – 175.00. The figurine in this set is very expensive and makes total price quite high. The figurine alone is shown on page 78. From the collection of Bev & Duane Brown.

CONSOLE SET. Bowl #1620 – 10", Candleholders #1619 – 4½", semi-matte salmon, scalloped-edged console set, $68.00 – 80.00.

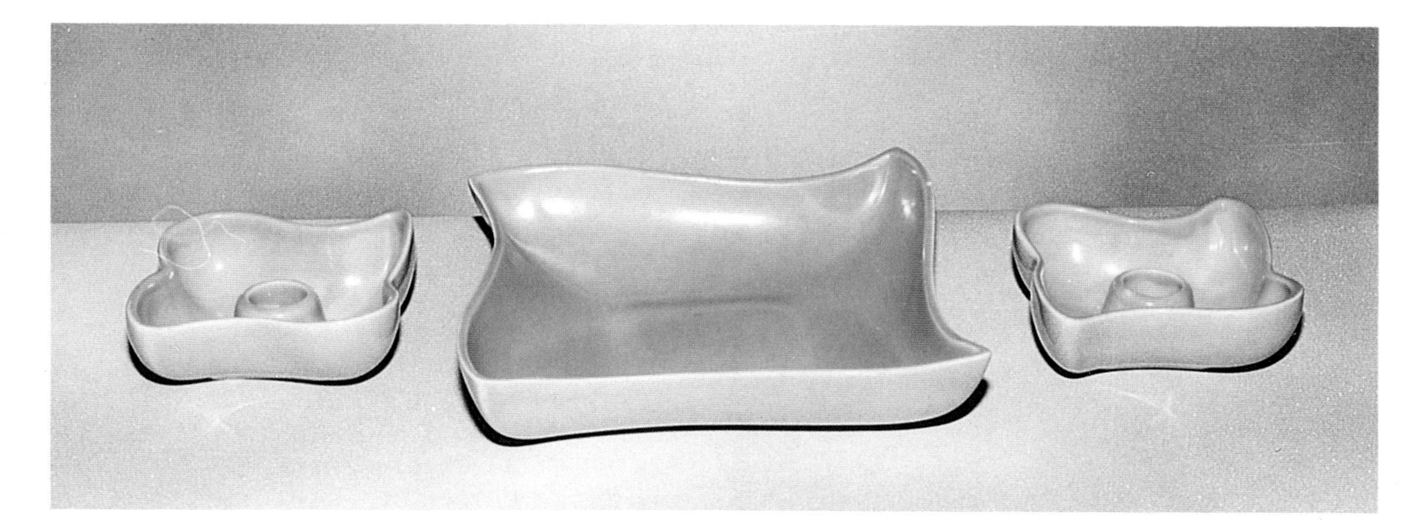

CONSOLE SET. Bowl #B1378 – 8", Candleholders B1411 – 4", gloss gray/coral petal shaped console set, $58.00 – 72.00.

Planters

PLANTER. #1378 – 5½", gloss gray/coral, square planter, $32.00 – 45.00.

PLANTER. #1552 – 6", fleck yellow/light green, shelf planter, $28.00 – 36.00.

PLANTER. #970 – 3½", gloss aqua, small rimmed planter, $24.00 – 36.00. These planters, produced since the 1940s, were called flowerpots in the early catalogs.

PLANTER. **#677 – 8½", gloss gray/coral, leaf embossed planter, $28.00 – 36.00.**

PLANTER. **#677 – 4½", gloss orange/light green, leaf embossed planter, $24.00 – 32.00. This planter style also came in a third size, 6½".**

PLANTER. **#432 – 13", gloss yellow/semi-matte brown, basket weave planter, $26.00 – 34.00.**

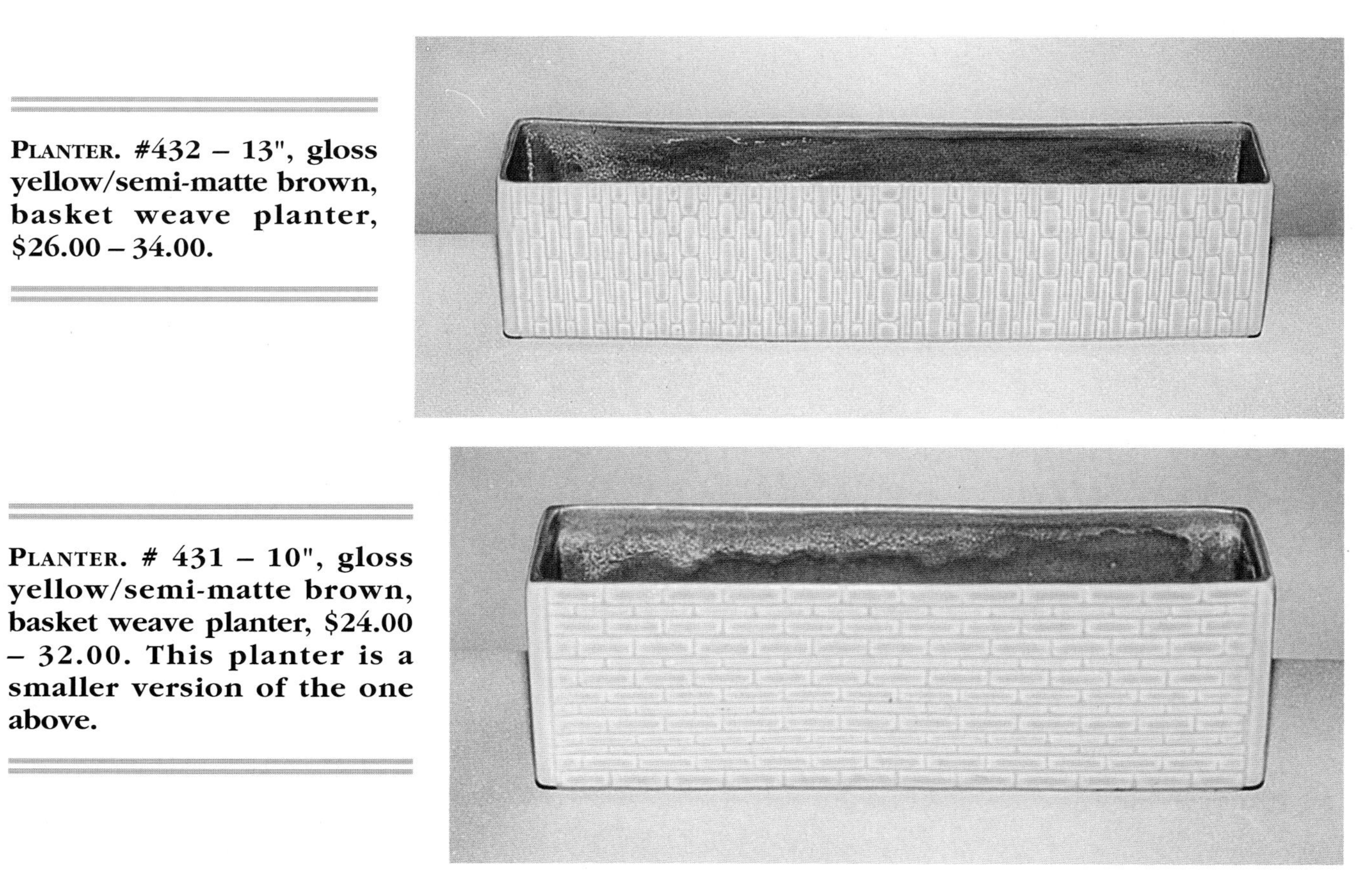

PLANTER. **# 431 – 10", gloss yellow/semi-matte brown, basket weave planter, $24.00 – 32.00. This planter is a smaller version of the one above.**

PLANTER. #643 – 4", gloss fleck zephyr pink, round embossed planter, $34.00 – 40.00.

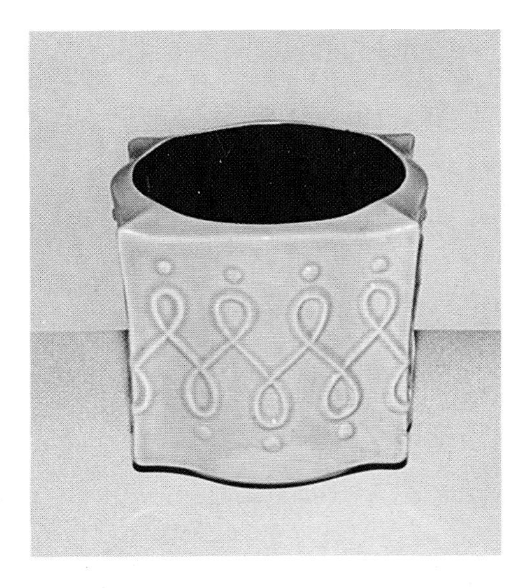

PLANTER. #1278 – 4½", gloss yellow/metallic brown, small embossed planter, $30.00 – 42.00. Art ware finished with the metallic brown color is hard to find. Quite attractive, it is also higher priced.

Wall Pockets

WALL POCKET. #M1630 – 10", semi-matte cypress green, funnel shaped wall pocket, $80.00 – 110.00. Very hard to find, any Red Wing wall pockets command high prices.

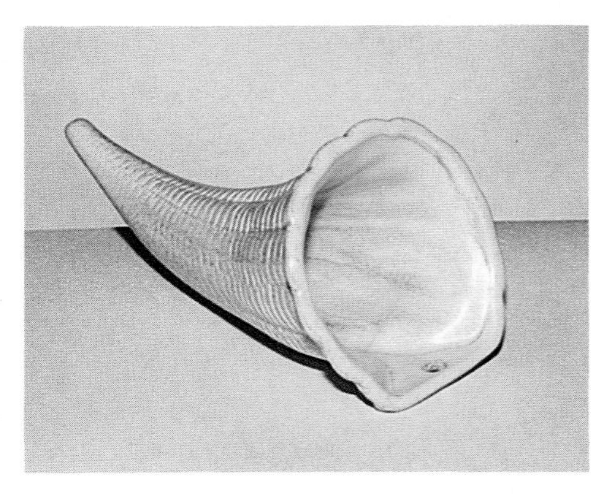

WALL POCKET. #441 – 6", gloss fleck Nile blue/colonial buff, cornucopia wall pocket, $75.00 – 90.00. This wall pocket matches the cornucopias that follow.

Cornucopias

Although harder to find than some of the other art ware, a collection of cornucopias would be quite unique. You could also add the cornucopia shaped vases produced earlier.

CORNUCOPIA. #443 – 10", gloss fleck Nile blue/colonial buff, cornucopia, $52.00 – 68.00.

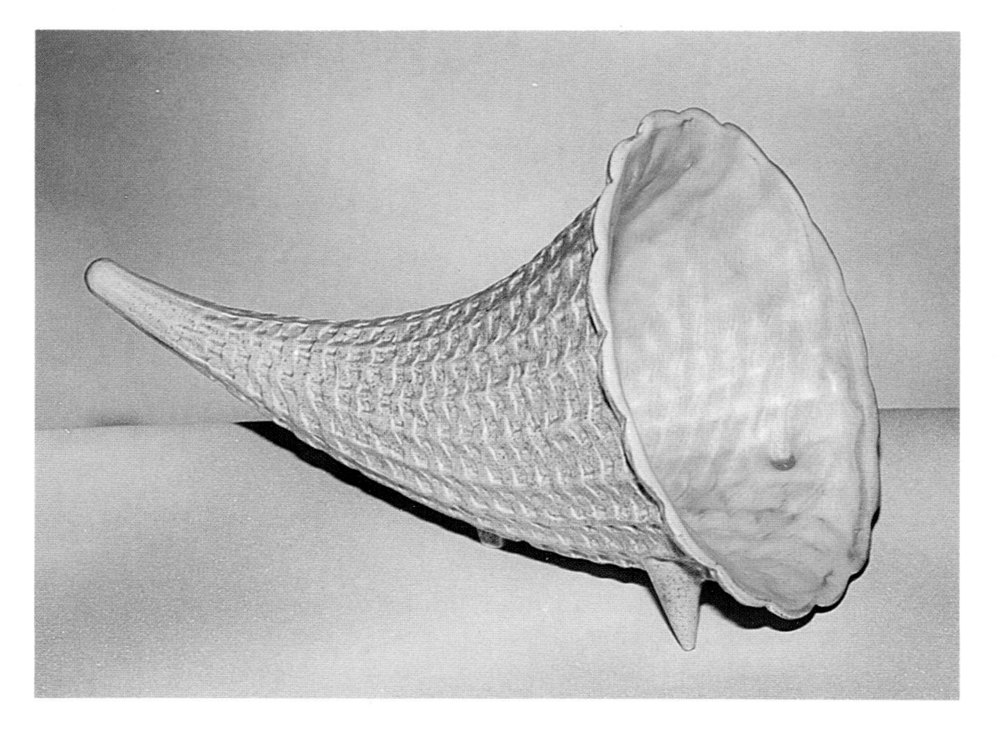

CORNUCOPIA. #442 – 15", gloss fleck Nile blue/colonial buff, cornucopia, $68.00 – 80.00.

Figurines

Figurines make a beautiful collection. They would also be good for those with limited storage or display space. They can be very expensive and quite hard to locate. There were many different people figurines, among them a cowboy, cherubs, a Madonna, and an Oriental man and woman.

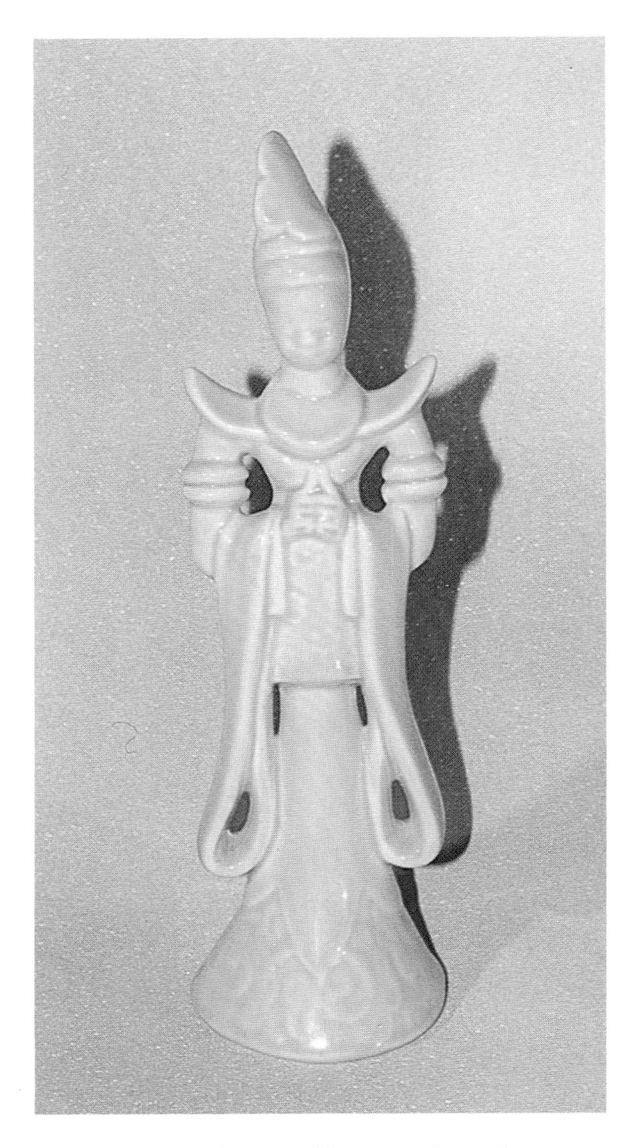

FIGURINE. #1308 – 10", gloss yellow, Oriental woman figurine, $100.00 – 130.00. There was a matching man figurine. From the collection of Bev & Duane Brown.

Art Pottery - 1960s

In the early 1960s, Red Wing continued grouping their art pottery by item in the catalogs. Most were called miscellaneous as in the 1950s. Some of the shapes from the past were carried on as had been done in previous years.

During this period Red Wing went back to the style of giving line names to their art pottery. This practice gave the art ware a certain distinction as with the older lines. Some of the new lines were Floraline, Stereoline, and Chromoline. They also introduced a new Decorator line and a Deluxe line in the 1960s. These lines were quite ornate like some of their earlier counterparts. Also introduced were a Prismatique line, a Belle line, and a Bronze line, all represented in this chapter.

The colors of the 1960s became brighter and more modern; Red Wing gave them specific names, such as cypress green, sagebrush, hyacinth, butterscotch, orchid, and coral. They also continued the basic colors that had been seen earlier.

The Red Wing catalogs of the 1950s and 1960s were produced in spring and fall editions. The shape number, description, size, and price of each piece were listed with pictures of the art ware. Colors were added or dropped between the spring and fall editions. Each piece at some time was produced in many different finish colors.

Like in the 1950s, the art ware continued to reflect the bright, contemporary look of the times, as well as some of the plainer more distinguished looking pottery. During this period Red Wing also continued producing their novelty planters.

Once you learn to recognize the look of the 1950s, you will also know the theme of the 1960s vintage. But you should always look at the bottom markings to identify the item as Red Wing.

Miscellaneous

As in previous years, there was a considerable amount of the art ware categorized as miscellaneous in the 1960s Red Wing catalogs. Both these miscellaneous pieces and the named lines are represented in the following photographs.

The Art Pottery in this chapter is from the author's collection unless otherwise noted.

Vases

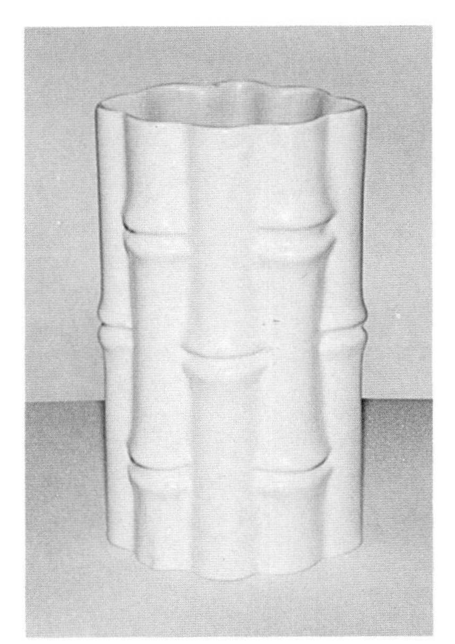

VASE. #1400 – 8", semi-matte white/green, bamboo motif vase, $30.00 – 42.00.

VASE. #1353 – 7½", semi-matte green/white, fancy leaf handled vase, $32.00 – 46.00.

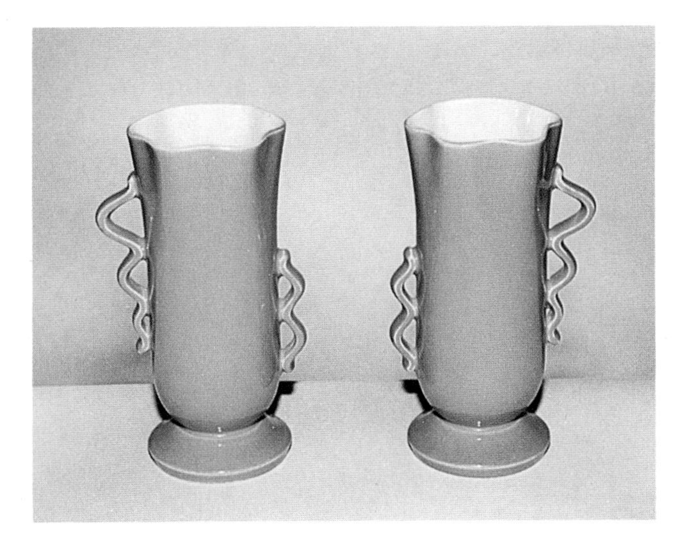

VASES. #1352 – 7½", gloss blue/yellow, double handled vases, $32.00 – 44.00 each. A pair of these vases was sold as part of a console set with bowl #1347 – 10½" (p. 82).

Vase. #687 – 15", semi-matte tan/ brown, floor vase, $54.00 – 68.00. This shape was also produced in the 1930s miscellaneous vases, and used again in the 1960s Chromoline. From the collection of Bev & Duane Brown.

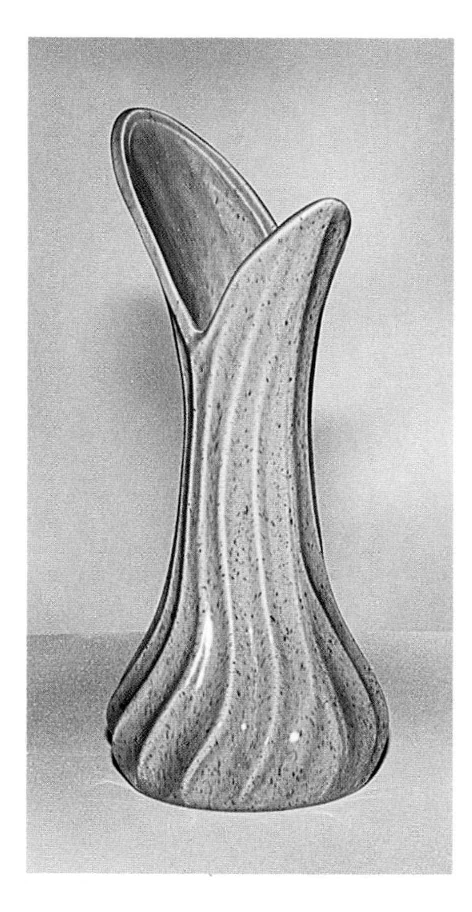

Vase. #818 – 12", gloss fleck Nile blue, vertical grooved vase, $52.00 – 64.00. Introduced in the spring 1963 Red Wing catalog, this vase was produced in a variety of colors. The colors listed in the spring 1963 catalog were cypress green, cocoa brown, blue, and matte white. From the collection of Bev & Duane Brown.

Vase. #B1399 – 5½", gloss yellow/gray, fan style vase, $38.00 – 46.00.

Vase. #819 – 12", gloss cinnamon, vertical grooved pitcher vase, $58.00 – 72.00. This vase was also introduced in the spring 1963 catalog along with #818 (p.81). Both vases were also listed in the 1964 and 1965 gift catalogs. From the collection of Bev & Duane Brown.

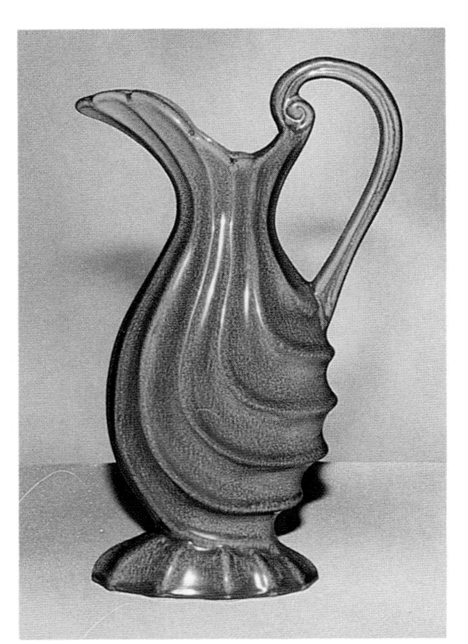

Bowl. #1347 – 10½", gloss blue/yellow, console bowl, $40.00 – 50.00. This bowl was part of a console set with a pair of #1352 – 7½" vases (p. 80).

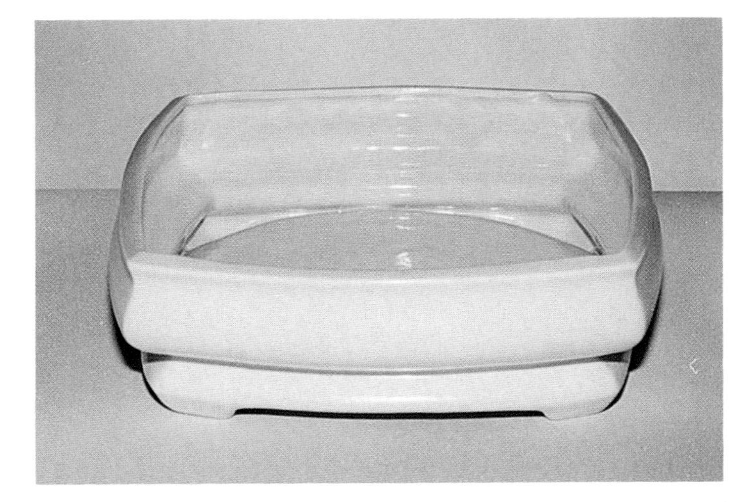

Bowl. #815 – 9", semi-matte white/green, square footed bowl, $38.00 – 46.00.

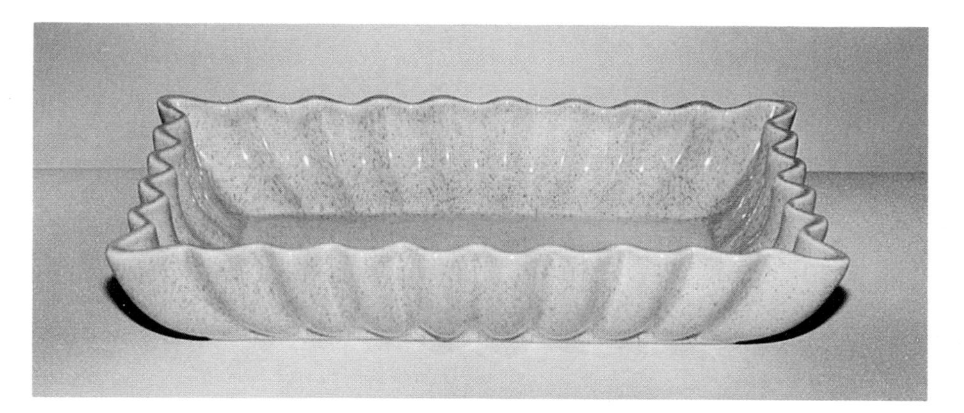

Bowl. #1309 – 12", gloss fleck zephyr pink, ribbed rectangular bowl, $42.00 – 54.00.

Bowl. #M1485 – 8", gloss cinnamon, ribbed triangle-footed bowl, $32.00 – 42.00.

Bowl. #M1603 – 10", gloss fleck yellow, rectangle footed bowl, $32.00 – 38.00.

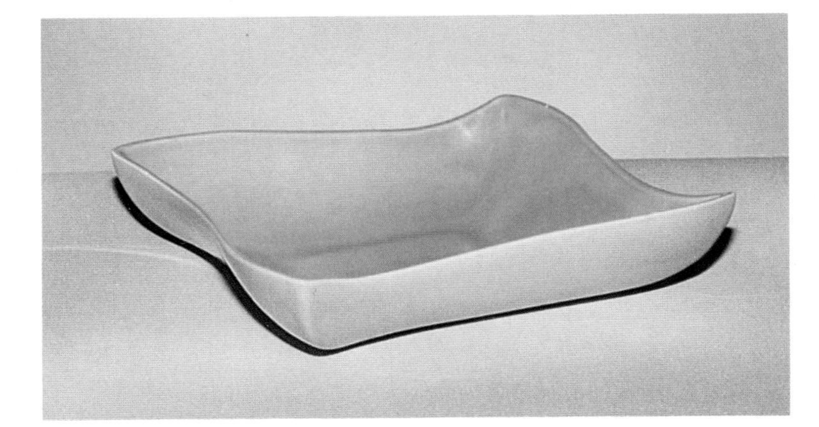

Bowl. #B1391 – 9", gloss gray/coral, petal shaped bowl, $30.00 – 38.00.

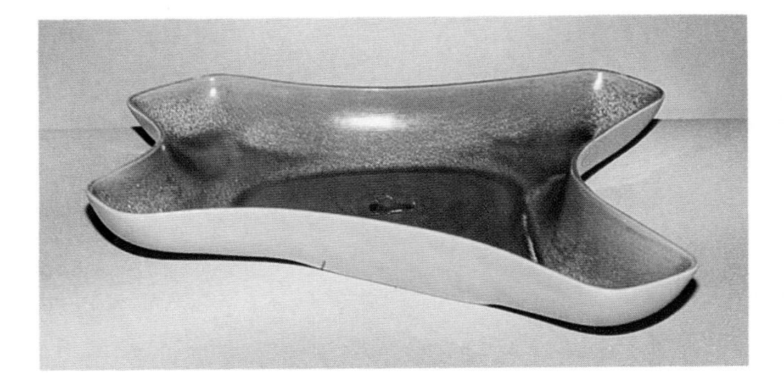

Bowl. #B1435 – 12", gloss yellow/semi-matte butterscotch, contoured bowl, $30.00 – 38.00.

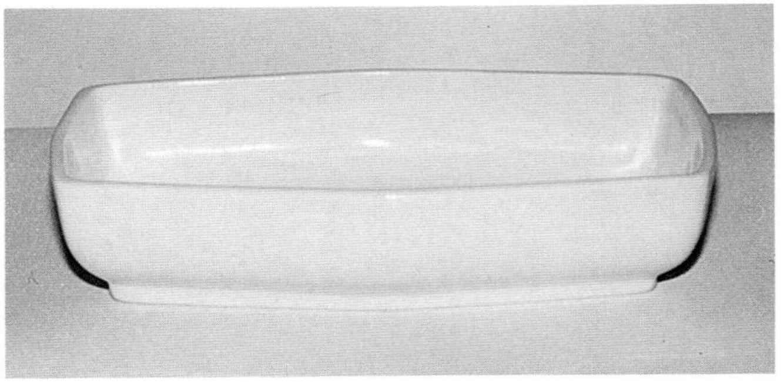

Bowl. #5019 – 9", semi-matte white, rectangular bowl, $30.00 – 38.00.

Bowl. #1381 – 7", semi-matte aqua/white, flower rimmed bowl, $32.00 – 40.00. This bowl is part of a large lazy Susan type set made up of four of #1380 – 9" pieces, positioned to form a circle with this bowl as the center. Each piece was sold separately in a 1964 Red Wing catalog which stated the pieces could be used as an ensemble or individually. This is a very attractive set.

Candleholders

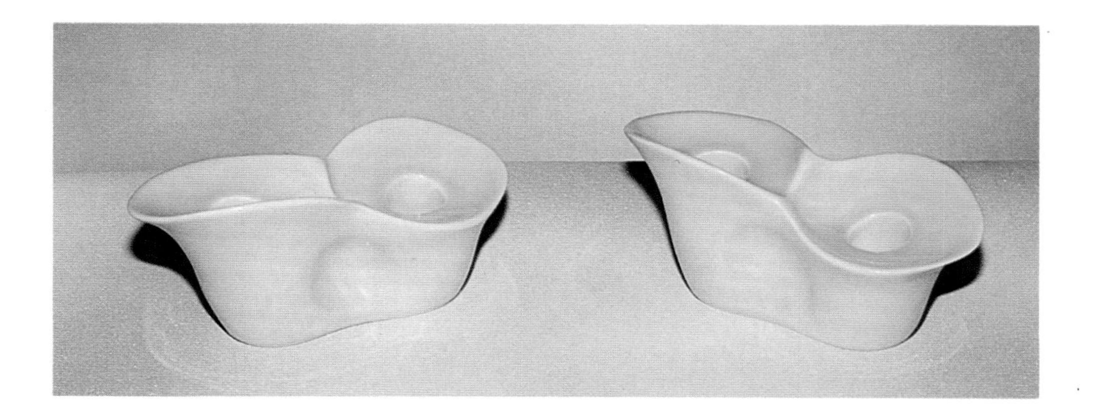

CANDLEHOLDERS. **#B1410 – 6", gloss yellow, double candleholders, $32.00 – 40.00 pair.**

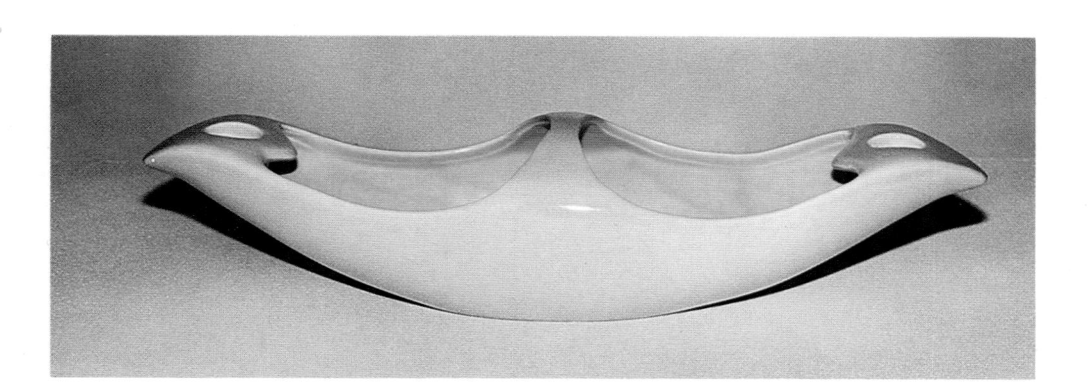

CANDLEHOLDER. **#B1420 – 10", gloss gray/coral, boat-shaped double candleholder, $32.00 – 40.00 each. This is a unique candleholder. A bowl type, it could hold flowers or other decorations. From the collection of Bev & Duane Brown.**

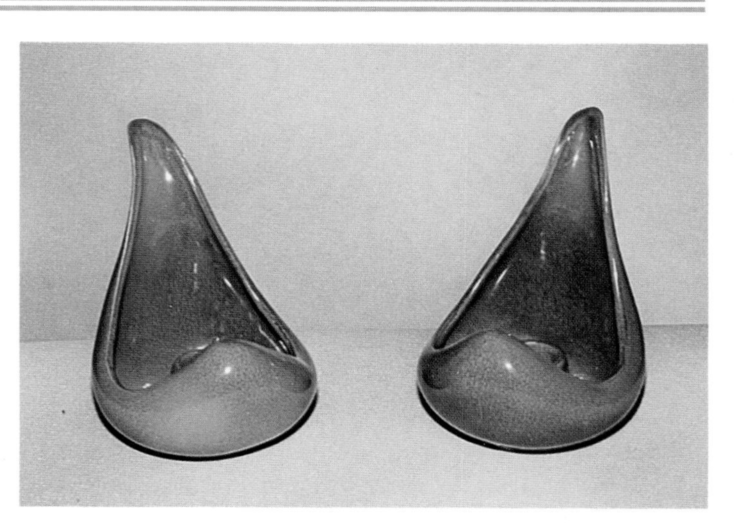

CANDLEHOLDERS. **#1409 – 5", gloss cinnamon, tear drop candleholders, $30.00 – 38.00 pair. On the pairs of candleholders, each is bottom marked with the shape number and Red Wing. Some of the Red Wing candleholders are not bottom marked.**

Console Sets

Console sets are not easily found. You will discover, however, that when you can find them, the price is usually lower than purchasing the pieces separately.

Console Set. Bowl #1304 – 13", Candleholders #B1410 – 6", gloss yellow/gray, console set, $60.00 – 72.00.

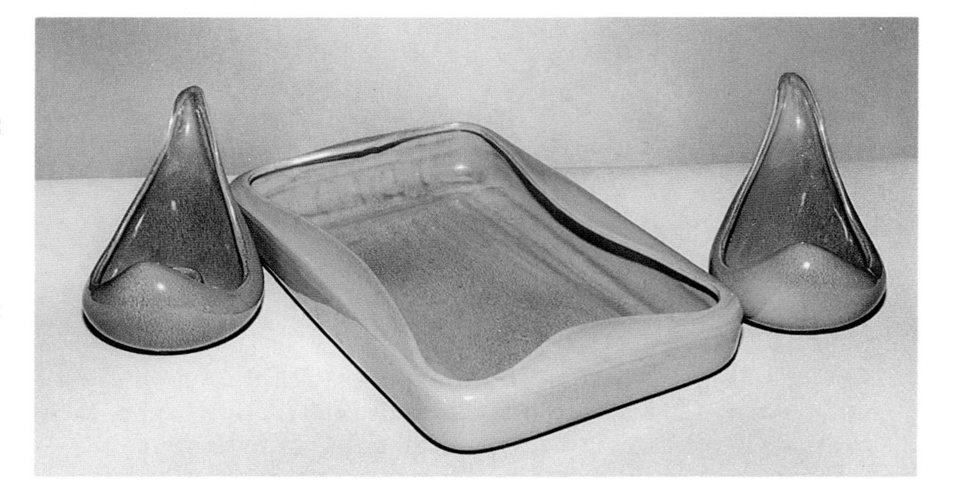

Console Set. Bowl #1348 – 12", Candleholders #1409 – 5", gloss cinnamon, console set, $58.00 – 68.00.

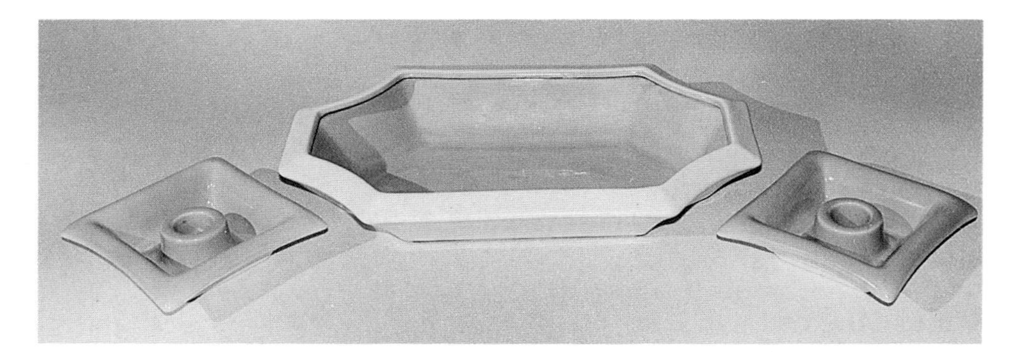

Console Set. Bowl #1307 – 10", Candleholders #1384 – 4½", semi-matte white/green, console set, $68.00 – 78.00. From the collection of Bev & Duane Brown.

PLANTER. #806 – 6", gloss fleck Nile blue/white, silver wing label, footed planter, $35.00 – 47.00.

Jardinieres

JARDINIERE. #110 – 10", semi-matte cypress green/yellow, pedestal jardiniere, $58.00 – 70.00. There were four sizes of these jardinieres; the smallest is pictured on the next page. They also were produced in shape #108 – 8", and #112 – 12". The size is the diameter of the item.

Jardiniere. #104 – 5½", gloss cocoa brown/yellow, pedestal jardiniere, $30.00 – 38.00. Listed in the fall 1962 Red Wing catalog, all the sizes were available in cypress green, cocoa brown, blue, black, and matte white.

Floraline

The Red Wing Floraline consisted of vases, bowls, compotes, candleholders, and planters produced in various finish colors. Many of them were also finished in two-tone colors. A list of some of the various colors of each era can be found at the end of this book.

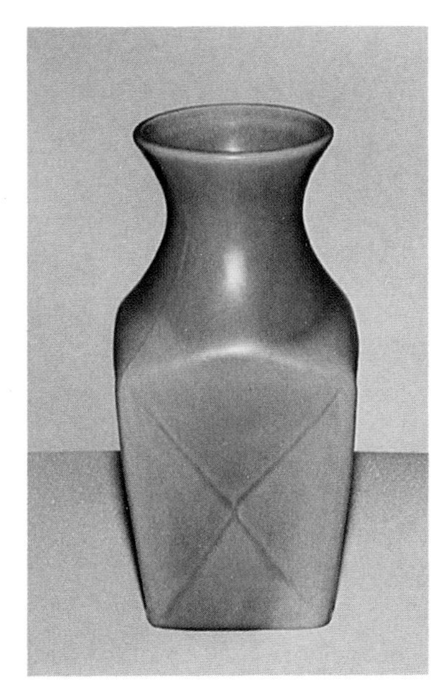

Vase. #1633 – 7", semi-matte cypress green, prism type vase, $38.00 – 48.00.

Vase. #1559 – 9½", gloss fleck green, pitcher vase, $34.00 – 46.00. Any of these fleck colors are harder to find and the pricing seems to be higher.

Vase. #1580 – 5", semi-matte black, pitcher vase, $42.00 – 58.00. An unusual vase not often found, so the price will be higher. The more unusual items are generally more expensive. From the collection of Bev & Duane Brown.

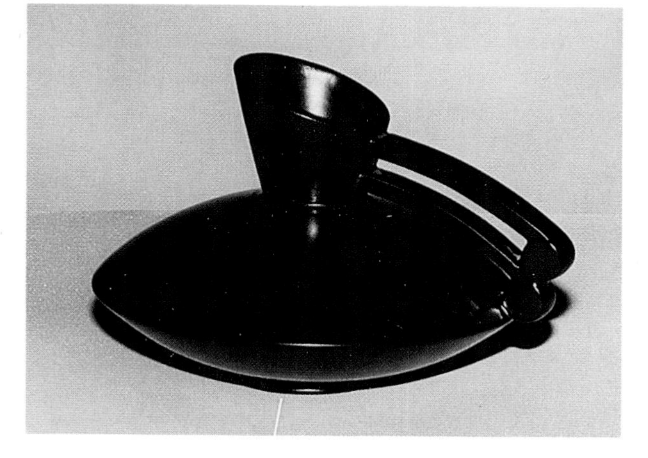

Vase. #416 – 12", semi-matte cinnamon/ light green, gladiolus vase, $62.00 – 75.00. Designed to hold gladiolas, this vase was produced in two sizes, both with the same shape number. It makes a beautiful display with the flower fanned across the vase. Below is the smaller size. Advertised in the spring 1961 Red Wing catalog, this vase sold for $5.50.

Vase. #416 – 10", semi-matte cinnamon, gladiolus vase, $50.00 – 60.00. Advertised in the 1964 Red Wing gift catalog, this vase sold for $4.50. Both sizes were available in cypress green, matte white, cinnamon, and black.

The following fan vases show the wide variety of color finishes that were used on the same shape of art ware. These fan vases would also make a lovely collection and can be found fairly easily in an array of colors.

VASE. #892 – 7½", semi-matte metallic brown/ Tahitian gold, fan vase, $42.00 – 52.00. From the collection of Bev & Duane Brown.

VASE. #892 – 7½", semi-matte blue/white, fan vase, $36.00 – 48.00. From the collection of Bev & Duane Brown.

VASE. #892 – 7½", gloss maroon/blue, fan vase, $52.00 – 62.00. A piece of art ware finished in the maroon color commands higher prices. From the collection of Bev & Duane Brown.

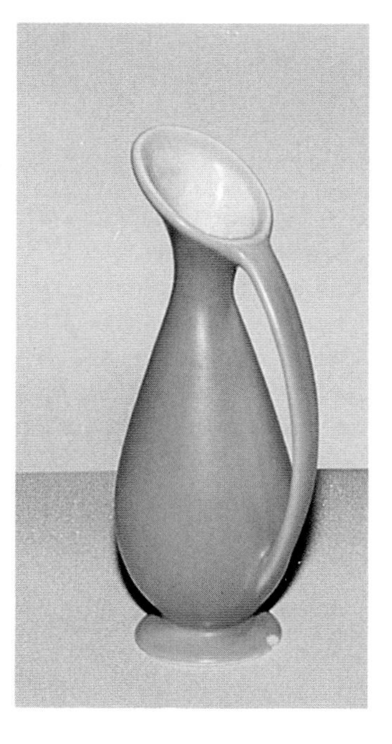

Vase. #M1510 – 7", semi-matte coral/tan, long handled bud vase, $28.00 – 40.00.

Compote. #M5008 – 6", semi-matte black, round compote, $42.00 – 54.00. From the collection of Bev & Duane Brown.

Compote. #761 – 6", semi-matte coral/yellow, cherub compote, $78.00 – 100.00. Very hard to find, these compotes are quite expensive. From the collection of Bev & Duane Brown.

Compote. **#761 – 6", semi-matte cypress green/yellow, cherub compote, $78.00 – 100.00. There are candleholders that match this compote. They look like the bottom of the compote with the cherubs on them. These candleholders are very scarce and would no doubt be expensive if found.**

Planter. **#B1403 – 5", semi-matte black, violet planter, $28.00 – 36.00. These planters, produced in a variety of colors, originally came with a common red clay insert to hold the plant.**

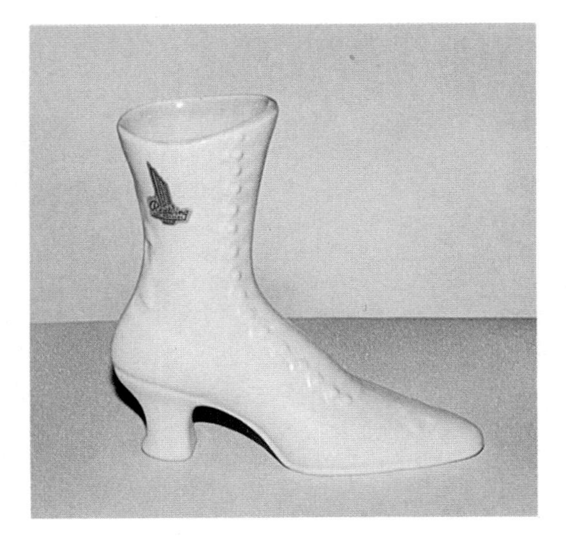

Planter. **#651 – 6", semi-matte white/ green, silver wing label, shoe planter, $60.00 – 80.00. Quite hard to find, any of the novelty planters commands high prices.**

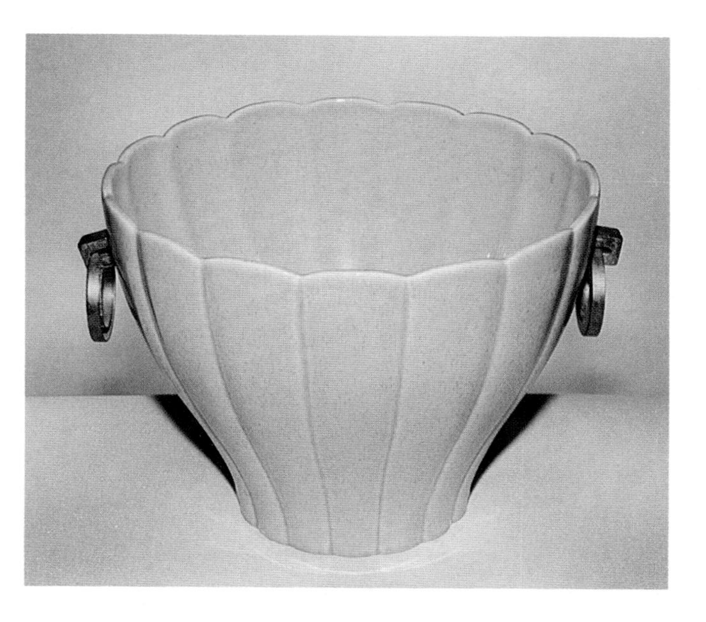

Jardiniere. #M1610 – 10", gloss fleck yellow, scallop top brass trimmed jardiniere, $48.00 – 62.00. This jardiniere was produced in five sizes, 4", 6", 8", 10", and 12". All the shapes were identical with the same shape number.

Jardiniere. #M1610 – 6", gloss fleck pink, scallop top jardiniere, $18.00 – 25.00. This jardiniere is missing the original brass handles, which reduces the price considerably. It is included to show the different size and color.

Stereoline

The Red Wing Stereoline consisted of vases, bowls, compotes, candleholders, planters, ashtrays, and jardinieres. Colors of the pottery were the same as Floraline. However, Red Wing continued to add new colors in every shade imaginable. By the mid 1960s there were many more colors than in previous years. Most of the Stereoline items were also available in the Decorator line colors, which were blue, silver green, and burnt orange.

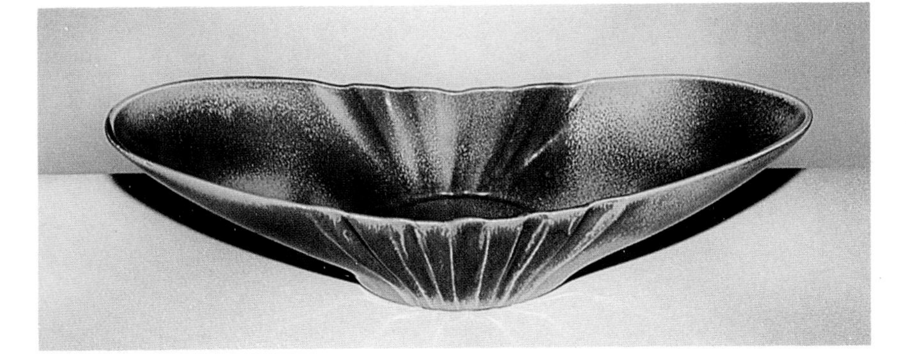

Bowl. #664 – 14", semi-matte hyacinth, elongated bowl, $34.00 – 40.00. This bowl is part of the Doric ensemble, which includes vases, compotes, candleholders, and this bowl. All the pieces have the same ribbed trim.

Compote. #764 – 13", semi-matte butterscotch, leaf handled compote, $36.00 – 42.00. There were also two urn vases that matched this compote. One of these is shown on page 104.

CANDLEHOLDERS. #661 – 6", gloss bitter-sweet, tall rimmed candleholders, $32.00 – 38.00 pair. These candleholders would match the bowl shown at top of opposite page. They are also part of the Doric ensemble. The vases look almost identical to the candleholders only taller.

CANDLEHOLDER. #678 – 6", gloss hyacinth, tapered candleholder, $28.00 – 34.00 pair.

CONSOLE SET. BOWL #664 – 14", Candleholder #678 – 6", semi-matte hyacinth, console set, $58.00 – 70.00 with a pair of candleholders. Although this candleholder is not part of the Doric ensemble, since it is the same color it looks fine with the bowl as a set. You will find that because of the many items produced in one finish color, it is easy to mix and match for sets.

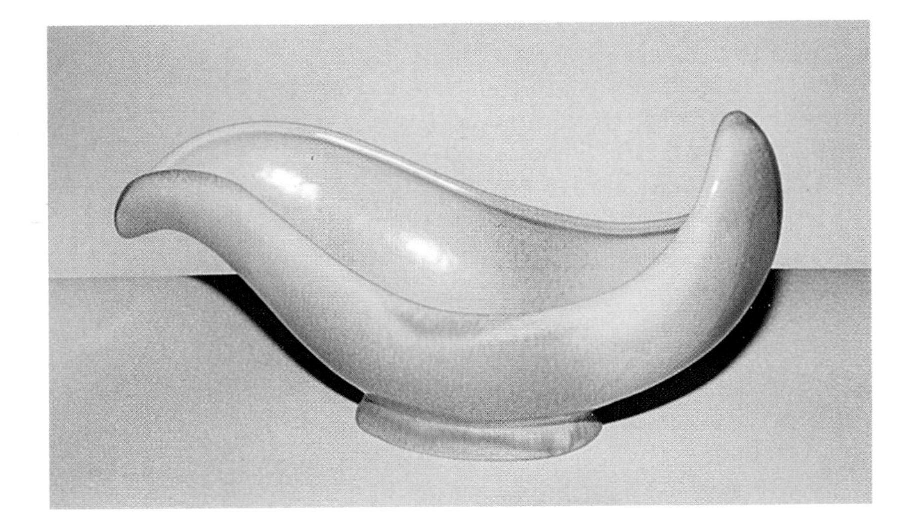

Planter. **#1582 – 10", semi-matte bronze green, oval planter, $30.00 – 36.00.**

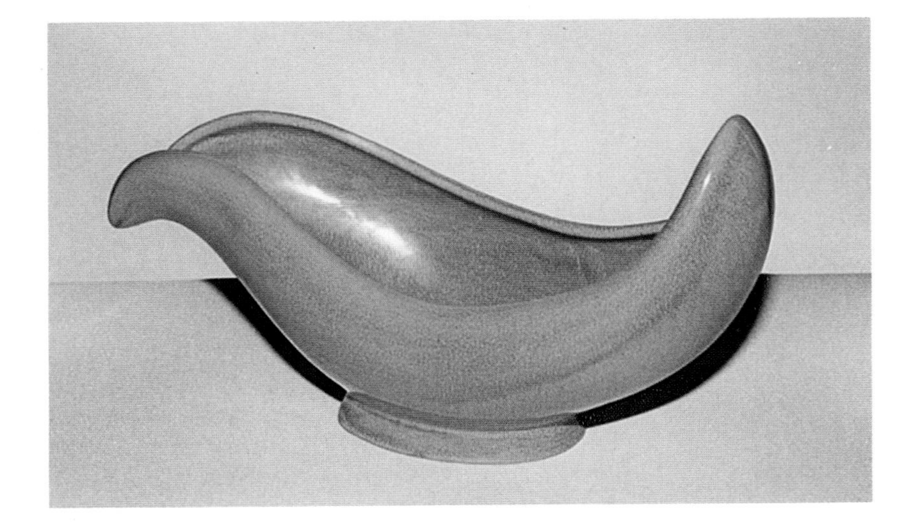

Planter. **#1582 – 10", semi-matte cinnamon, oval planter, $30.00 – 36.00.**

Textura Line

The Textura line was produced in various shaped vases, bowls, and planters. There were also a bird figurine and candleholders, called candlesticks in the spring 1963 Red Wing catalog. Like the other Red Wing art ware, the Textura was produced in many different color combinations.

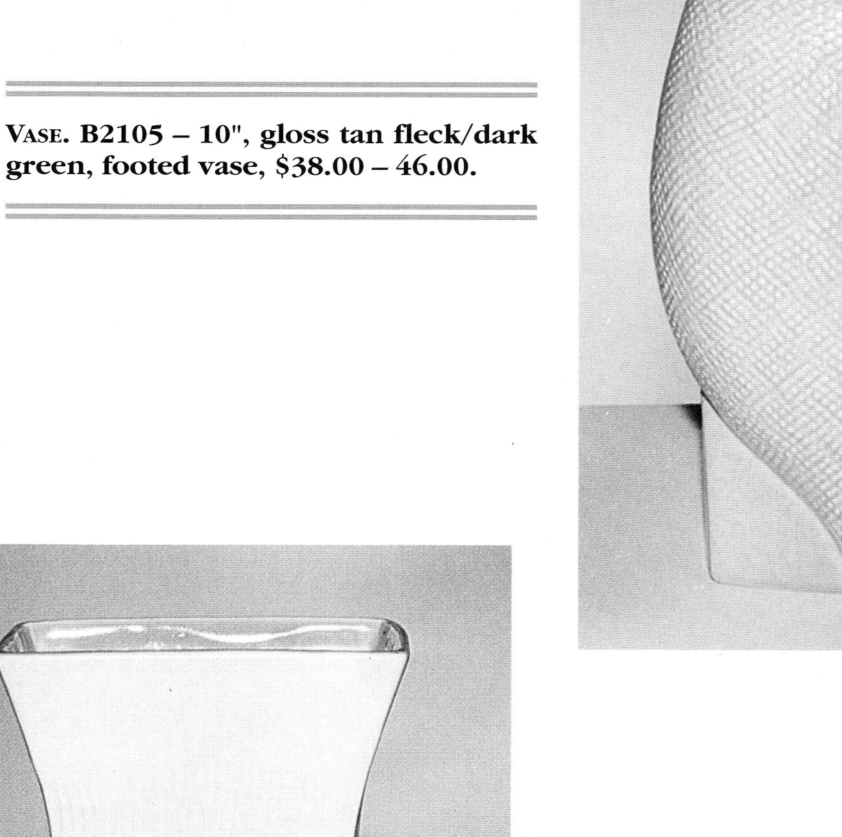

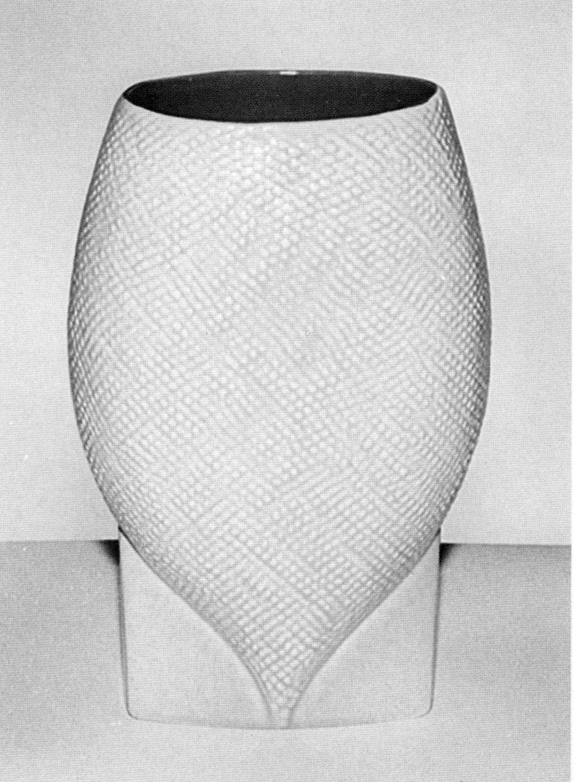

VASE. B2105 – 10", gloss tan fleck/dark green, footed vase, $38.00 – 46.00.

VASE. #B2100 – 8", semi-matte white/ green, curved vase, $38.00 – 48.00. Although hard to see, this vase has the textured finish on the front which is characteristic of the Textura line. From the collection of Bev & Duane Brown.

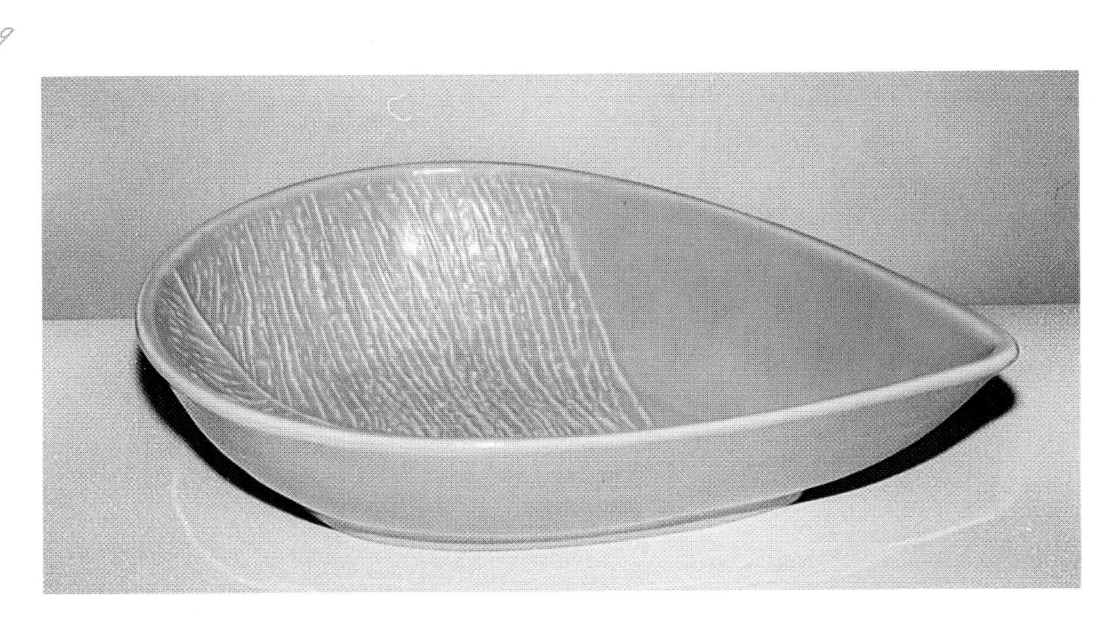

Bowl. #B2108 – 11¼", gloss gray/coral, tear drop bowl, $32.00 – 42.00.

Bowl. #B2109 – 12¼", gloss gray/coral, rectangular bowl, $32.00 – 42.00.

Planter. #B2101 – 8", gloss gray/coral, rectangular planter, $32.00 – 40.00.

Prismatique Line

The Prismatique line was very modern and eye catching, having distinguished geometrical prism shapes glazed with bright colors. The line consisted of vases, bowls, compotes, and planters. Some were rounded and others had straight lines.

The Prismatique line was advertised in the 1964 Red Wing gift catalog as smartly styled pieces of art pottery with a color treatment that is both beautiful and unique. Some of the colors are in the color chart at the end of this book.

Prismatique art ware is becoming very popular, not only with the Red Wing collectors, but also with those who collect Art Deco pottery. Therefore, the prices have been on the rise for the past several years. This line is not easily found in some locations.

The following items show some of the color combinations and the two styles of Prismatique.

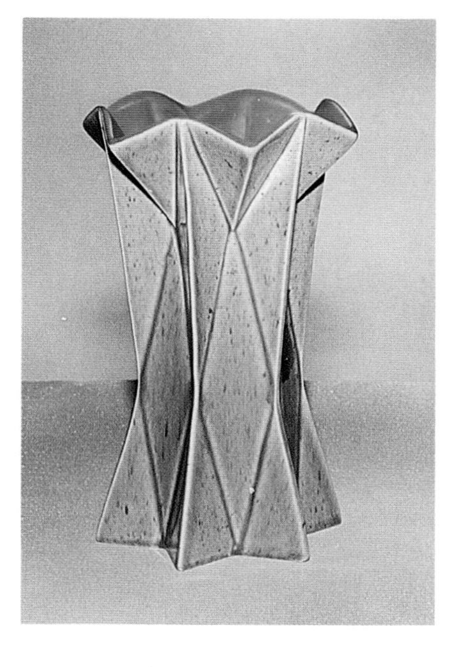

VASE. #798 – 8", gloss celadon/mandarin orange, medium vase, $60.00 – 74.00. Belle Kogan designed this line. From the collection of Bev & Duane Brown.

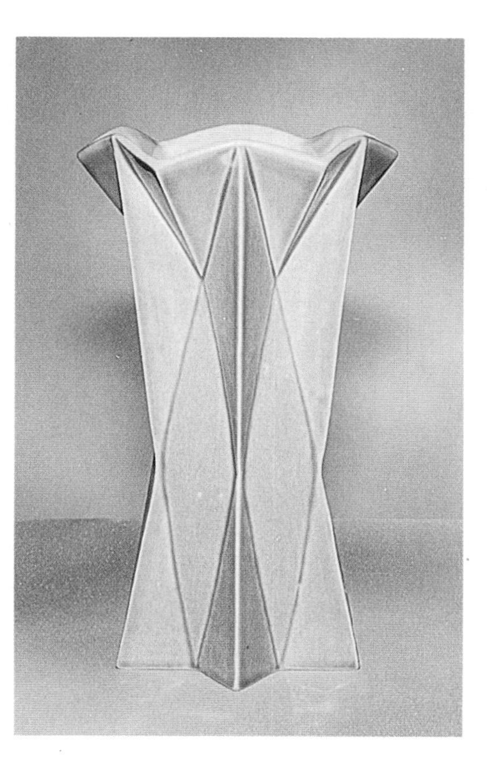

VASE. #797 – 11", gloss Persian blue/white, tall vase, $68.00 – 82.00. This is an example of the straight angle style. From the collection of Bev & Duane Brown.

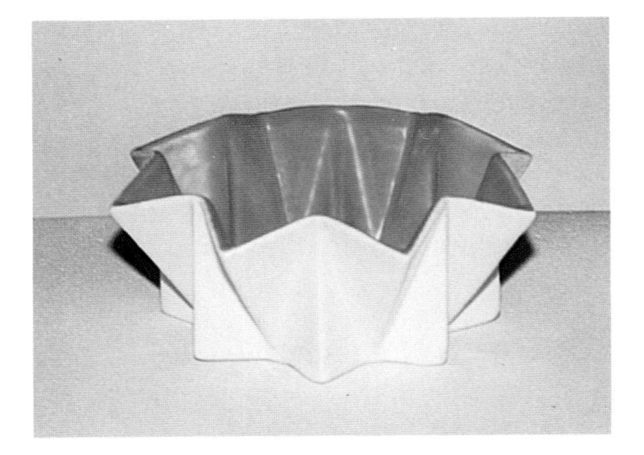

Bowl. #791 – 6½", gloss white/mandarin orange, small bowl, $38.00 – 46.00.

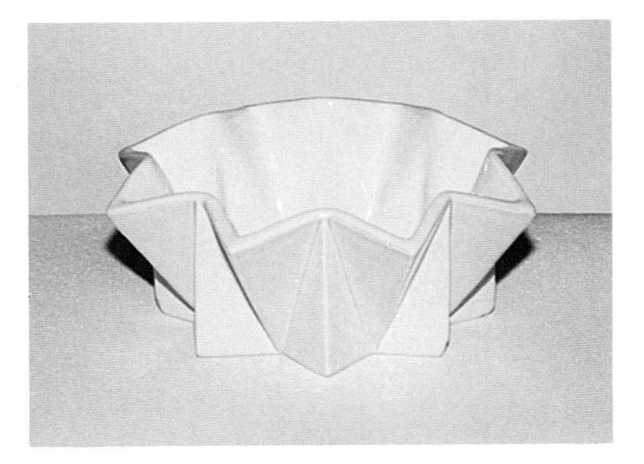

Bowl. #791 – 6½", gloss Persian blue/white, small bowl, $38.00 – 46.00.

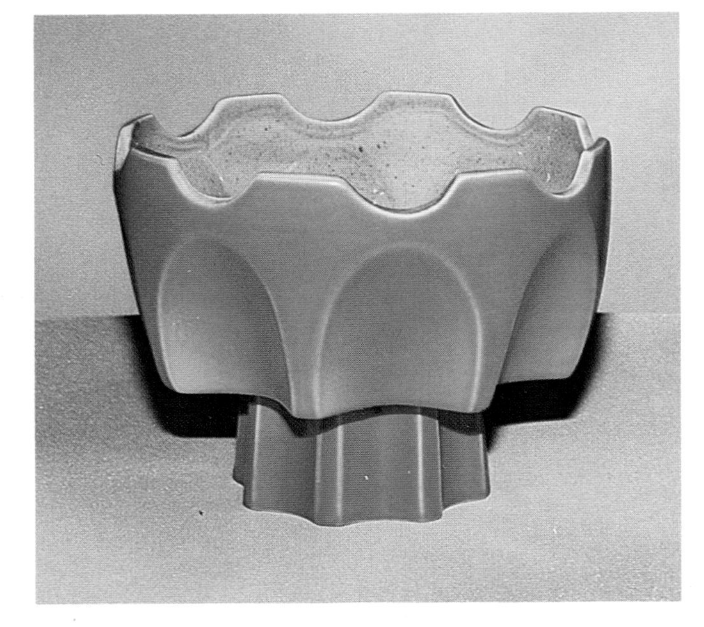

Compote. #788 – 5½", semi-matte mandarin orange/celadon, low footed, rounded style compote, $56.00 – 68.00. In a 1964 gift catalog, Red Wing sold the Prismatique vases in one color combination, and advertised that the colors on the bowl, planter, and compotes were reversed. Red Wing always maintained a policy of changing colors on the art ware from season to season, and as stated in this catalog, reversing colors on the different shapes. Not all colors were available in a different season's catalog.

Tropicana Line

Named for its tropical look, the Tropicana line came in a variety of vases, bowls, and planters. There were also a candelabra and a 13" window box bowl. The art pottery was produced in various two-tone finishes, and all were decorated in one of three embossed styles. There was Desert Flower, Shell Ginger, and Bird of Paradise.

Tropicana art ware is not plentiful, but can be found. This line is known to have been sold in the 1963 and 1964 Red Wing catalogs.

The following pictures show each of the three decorating styles and some of the color combinations.

VASE. #B2007 – 12", gloss metallic brown/yellow, Shell Ginger vase, $42.00 – 54.00. From the collection of Bev & Duane Brown.

VASE. #B2004 – 10", gloss dark green/yellow, Desert Flower Vase, $38.00 – 46.00.

Vase. #B2005 – 8", gloss yellow/dark green, Shell Ginger vase, $36.00 – 46.00. The B preceding the shape number on all of the Tropicana items indicates Belle Kogan designed this line.

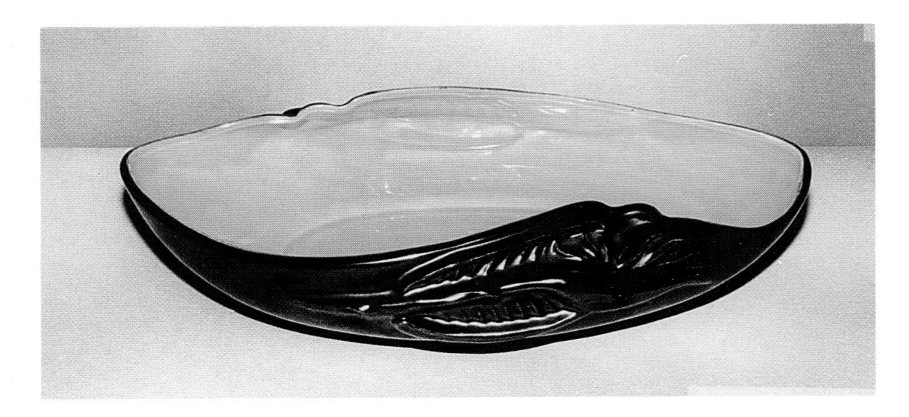

Bowl. #B2014 – 14", gloss metallic brown/yellow, Bird of Paradise bowl, $40.00 – 54.00.

Console Set. Vase #B2005 – 8", Candleholders #B2505 – 4½", gloss yellow/ dark green console set, $62.00 – 78.00. The candleholders in this set are not Tropicana; they are Deluxe Line, Ivy. This set was put together simply to show Red Wing color finishes throughout the years will mix and match to form whatever type of setting you desire.

Belle Line

The Belle line was produced in various shapes of vases, bowls, and compotes. There was also at least one pair of candlesticks. These pieces were finished in various colors and two different glazes, one a textured glaze, rough to the touch, the other a smooth gloss. The art ware was ribbed at the bottom with a smooth collar at the top of each piece, giving a contemporary look. There does not seem to be much of this pottery for sale in many areas.

The following pieces give a look at the style of this line. Other colors are listed in the color chart at the end of the book.

Bowl. #881 – 8", matte snow white/orange, silver wing label, low oval bowl, $32.00 – 40.00.

Bowl. #881 – 8", matte chocolate with white overlay/gold, low oval bowl, silver wing label, $32.00 – 40.00. These are examples of the textured matte glaze used on the Belle Line. The gloss glaze finish is smooth to the touch.

Bronze Line

A very decorative line, the Bronze line was produced in various ornate vases, compotes, urns, and candleholders. There is a wine pitcher, and pitcher vase, along with a pair of tear drop shaped candleholders, and a single totem pole style candleholder for a large diameter candle.

Some of the art ware was a solid bronze color, others two-tone. The following examples are the two-tone finish. Art ware from this line is not often found.

VASE. #763 – 8", gloss bronze/Tahitian gold, leaf handled urn vase, $56.00 – 70.00. This vase was pictured in a 1965 Red Wing catalog advertised under the Bronze Line, and sold for $5.25 each. The same shape number was listed elsewhere in the catalog under vases. Sold in cypress green, cocoa brown, blue, and matte white for $3.50 each. Comparison indicates that the Bronze Line was special and quite expensive for the times.

VASE. #947 – 5½", gloss bronze/Tahitian gold, cup style vase, $48.00 – 58.00. The actual color on this art ware is lighter and more of a bronze but appears darker in these pictures, almost a gun metal color.

Deluxe Line

Shown in a spring 1963 Red Wing catalog, the Deluxe line was one of the more ornate groups produced in the 1960s. The line shown in the 1963 catalog was two sets. Each set consisted of a bowl, a pair of candlesticks, and a figurine. One set had a shell theme, the other an ivy theme.

The swan figurine from the ivy set was shown at the 1995 Red Wing convention under rare items. These deluxe sets are very hard to find.

BOWL. #B2504 – 14½", gloss fleck pastel green, ivy bowl, $68.00 – 80.00. The other bowl in this line was a shell shape #B2501 – 13".

CANDLEHOLDERS. #B2505 – 4½", gloss fleck pastel green, ivy candleholders, $42.00 – 54.00 pair. The shell motif candleholders were horizontal shells #B2502 – 4½".

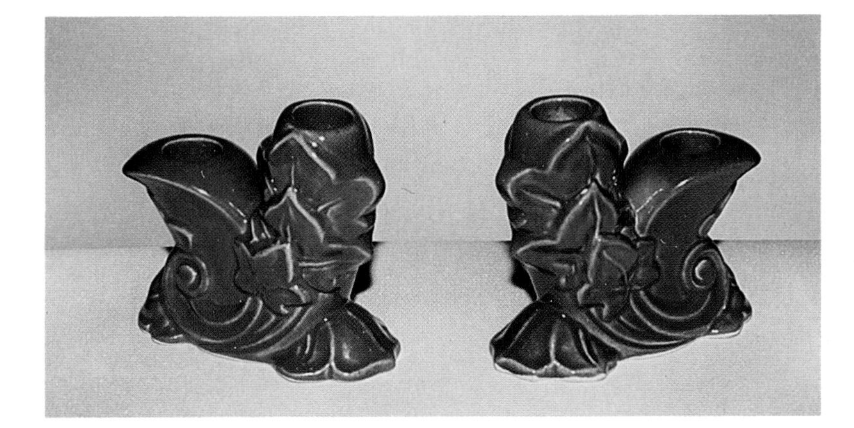

CANDLEHOLDERS. #B2505 – 4½", gloss dark green, ivy candleholders, $42.00 – 54.00 pair.

FIGURINE. #B2506 – 9", gloss fleck pastel green, swans figurine, $135.00 – 165.00. The figurine for the shell motif consisted of a wave with four stacked dolphins jumping over the wave.

CONSOLE SET. BOWL #B2504 – 14½", Candleholders #B2505 – 4½", Figurine #B2506 – 9", gloss fleck pastel green, Deluxe Line Ivy console set, $245.00 – 298.00. The shell console set is also very attractive. It, too, is extremely hard to find, and pricing is comparable.

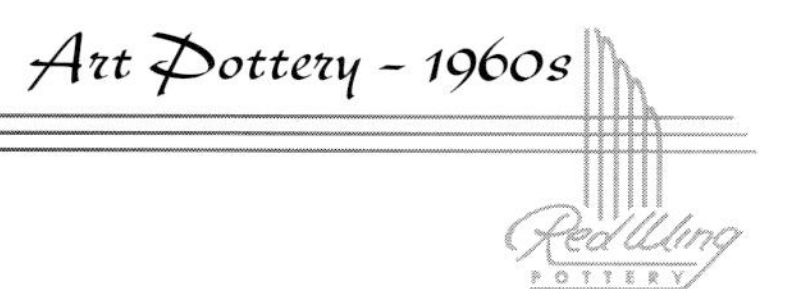

Garden Club Bowls

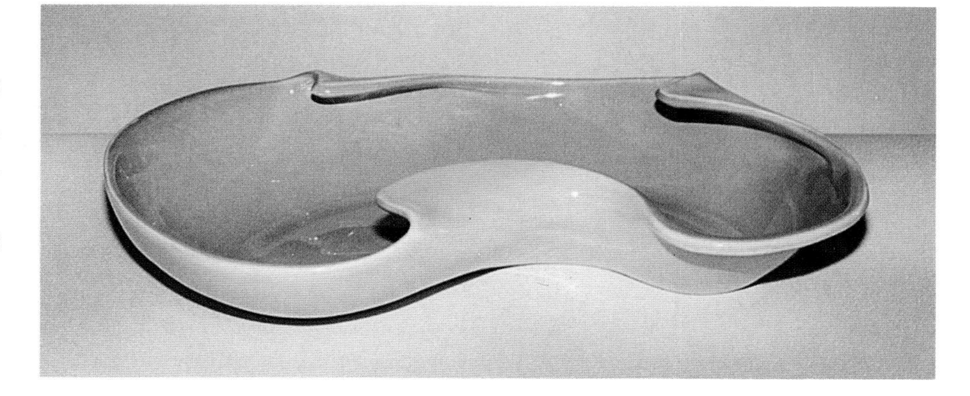

Bowl. #1304 – 13", gloss yellow/gray, contoured bowl, $34.00 – 42.00.

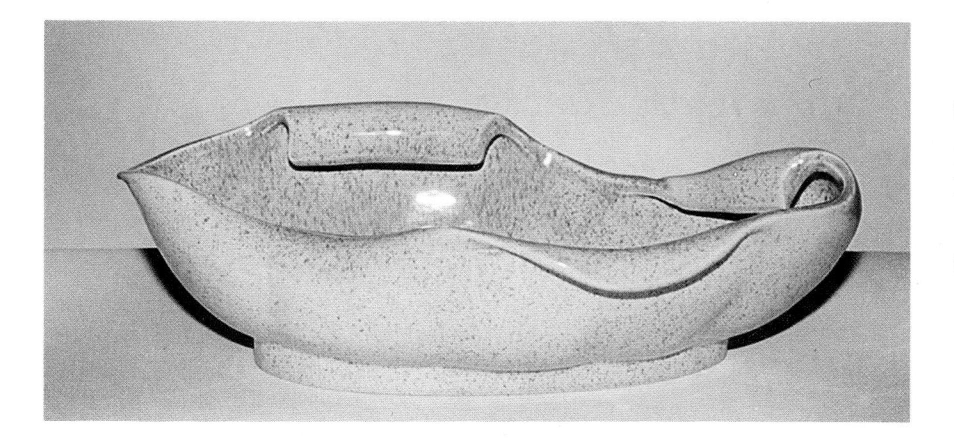

Bowl. #M1463 – 12", gloss fleck Nile blue, curled edge bowl, $38.00 – 48.00.

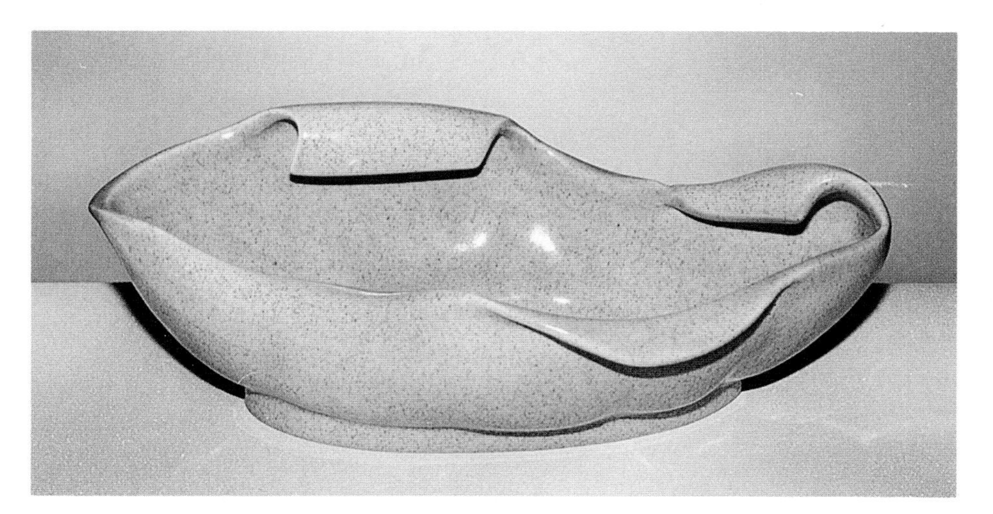

Bowl. #M1463 – 12", gloss fleck zephyr pink, curled edge bowl, $38.00 – 48.00. The M preceding these shape numbers indicates that Charles Murphy designed these bowls.

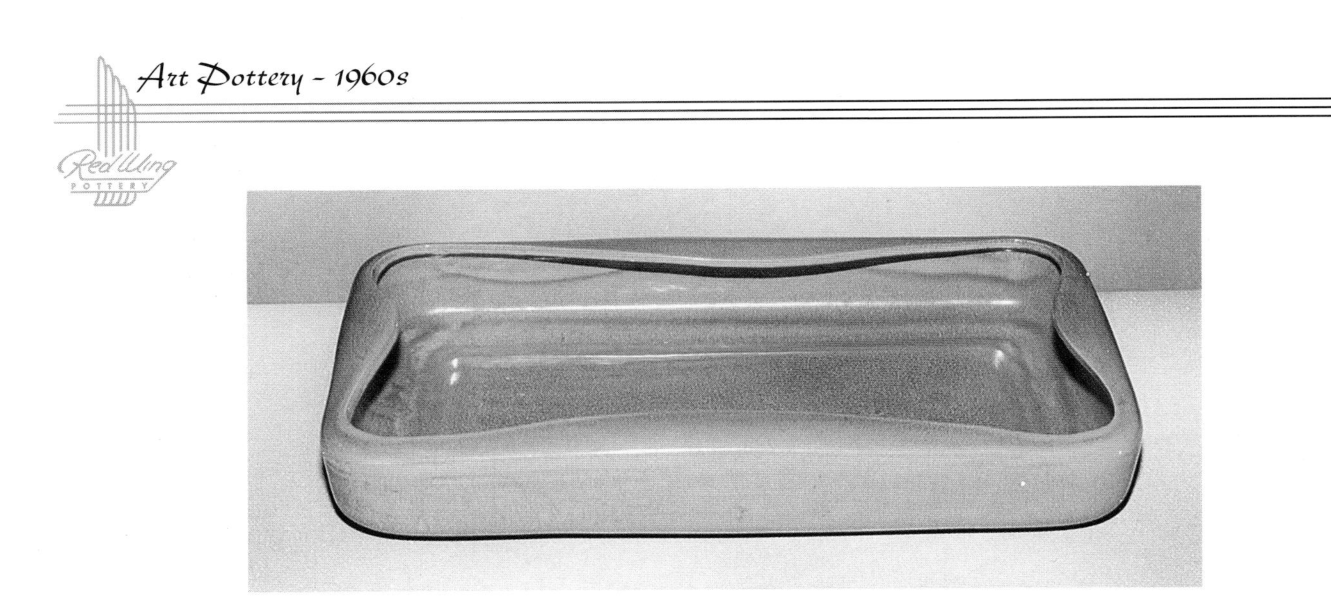

Bowl. #1348 – 12", semi-matte cinnamon, rectangular bowl, $34.00 – 42.00.

Window Box Bowls

Bowl. #407 – 12", gloss orange/tan, bamboo embossed bowl, $32.00 – 40.00. Notice the flat edge of this bowl, formed to set against a wall or window.

Bowl. #1429 – 10", gloss dark green/yellow, leaf-shaped bowl, $32.00 – 40.00.

Ashtrays

Red Wing produced a variety of ashtrays throughout their art pottery days. During the 1930s and 1940s Red Wing produced several types of ashtrays and what they called ash receivers. One of the ash receivers was shaped like a pelican and looked much like a figurine. The ashtrays were ornate and looked much like small art pottery bowls or shell dishes. There was an ashtray produced in the Magnolia line and some that were cigarette holders and ashtrays combined. These early pieces are rare and very hard to find.

Starting in the 1950s and 1960s, the ashtrays were produced in many different styles, most shaped like traditional ashtrays. During this period or perhaps sooner, Red Wing produced the famous maroon color wing ashtray, shaped like the Red Wing symbol. It is difficult to determine the vintage of the traditional ashtrays unless they were produced for a special occasion and dated. However, most have the 1950s and 1960s era look.

On the following pages you will see the famous Minnesota Twins and wing ashtrays, also a sample of some of these later ashtrays. You will be able to find some of the later types while you are looking for art pottery. You can also find the wing and Twins ashtrays with some looking.

Common

Ashtray. #M3005 – 11", gloss gold/brown, large square ashtray, $28.00 – 36.00. This ashtray looks identical except for color to the Decorator Line crystalline glazed ashtrays; the shape number is the same.

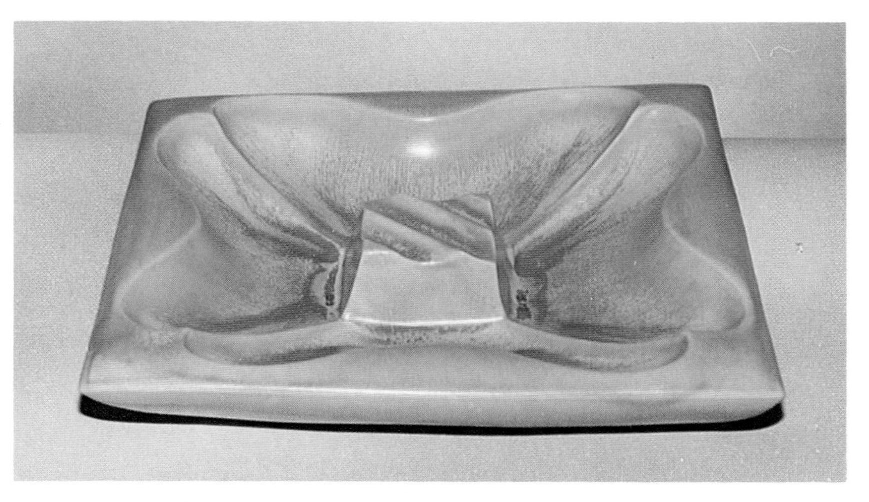

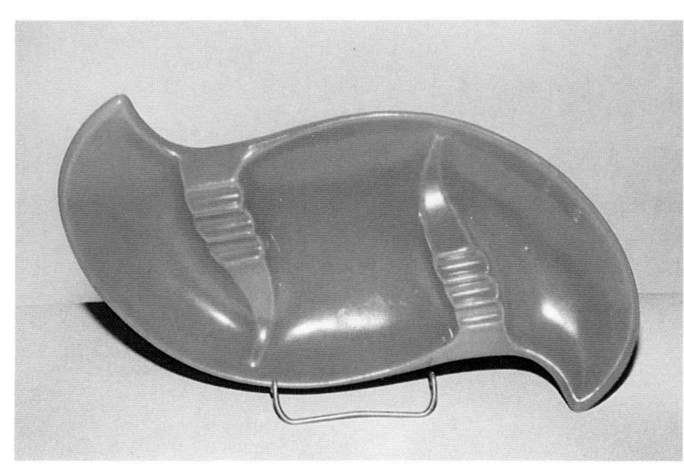

Ashtray. #745 – 6", gloss radiant orange, contoured ashtray, $24.00 – 30.00.

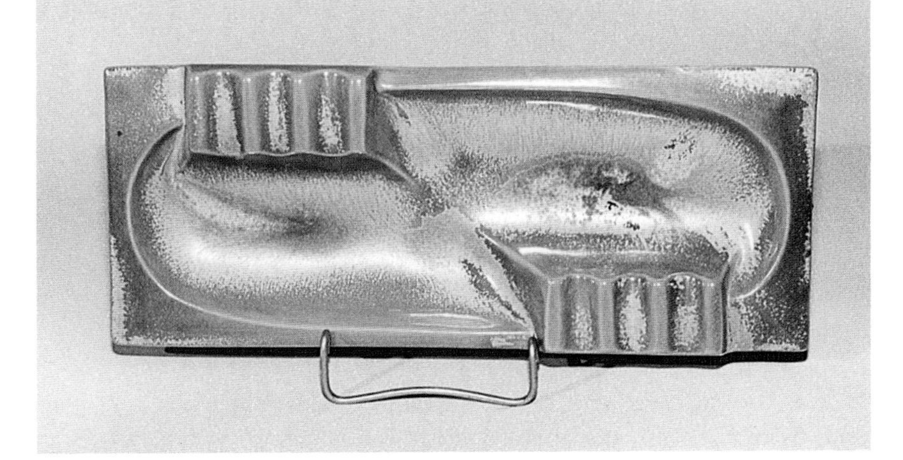

Ashtray. #3002 – 12", gloss silver green, rectangular ashtray, $24.00 – 32.00.

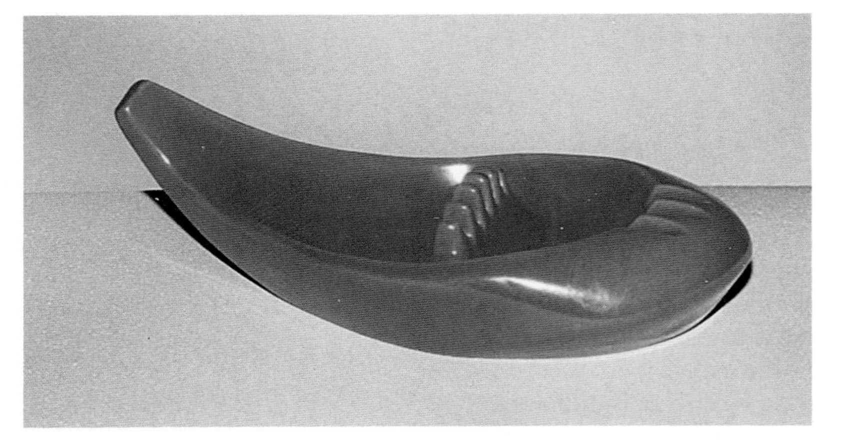

Ashtray. #774 – 6", gloss radiant orange, teardrop-shaped ashtray, #22.00 – 28.00.

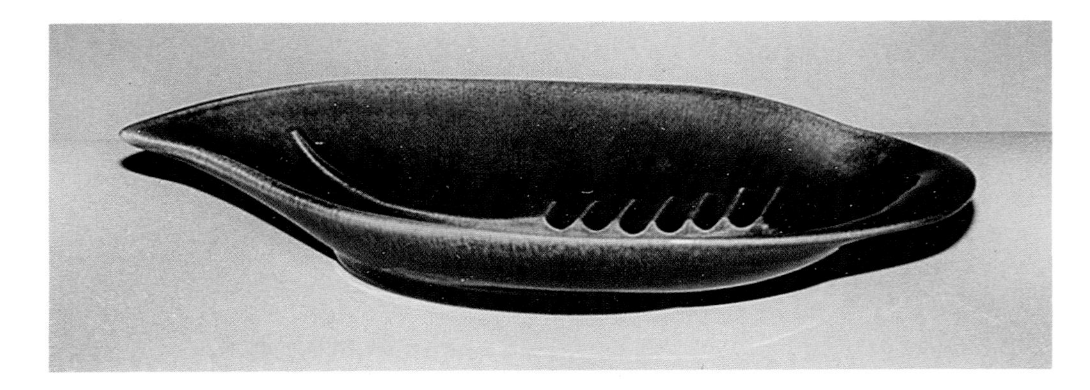

Ashtray. #746 – 9", gloss bronze green, leaf style ashtray, $22.00 – 30.00.

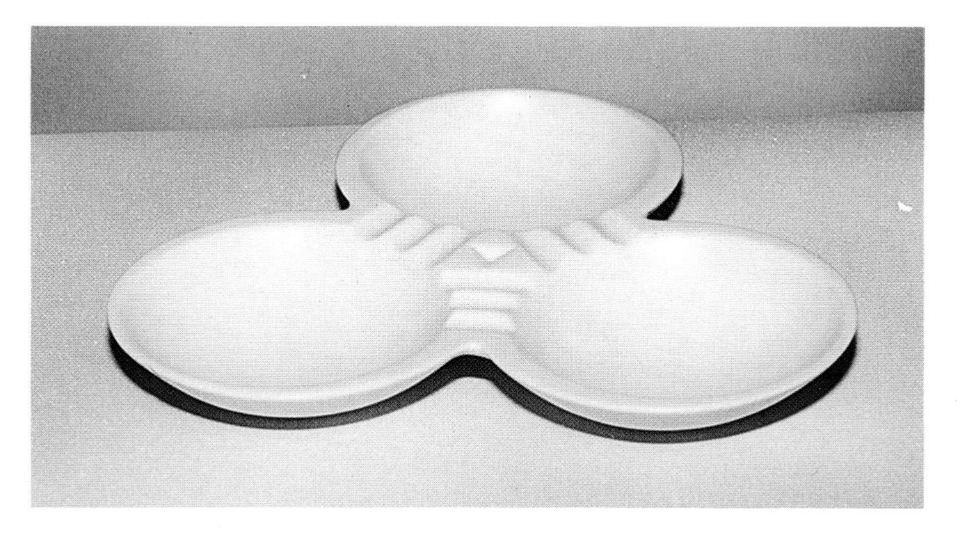

Ashtray. #742 – 9", semi-matte white, circle ashtray, $45.00 – 60.00. Notice the unusual shapes of these ashtrays.

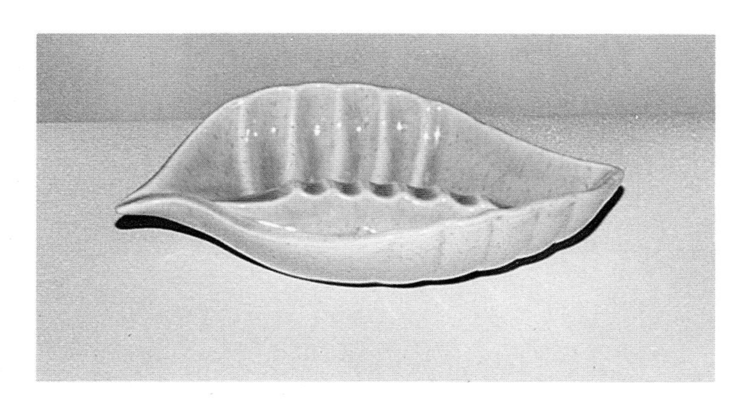

Ashtray. #739 – 5", gloss fleck orchid, leaf ashtray, $20.00 – 28.00.

Minnesota Twins

The following pictures show the famous Minnesota Twins ashtray. Produced in 1965 for the World Series and shaped like a baseball, this piece of art ware is very detailed. You will not find many of these for sale.

ASHTRAY. Bottom marked Red Wing Potteries U.S.A., gloss brown/green, Minnesota Twins baseball ashtray, $145.00 – 185.00. Below is the bottom view of the ashtray; notice the detail.

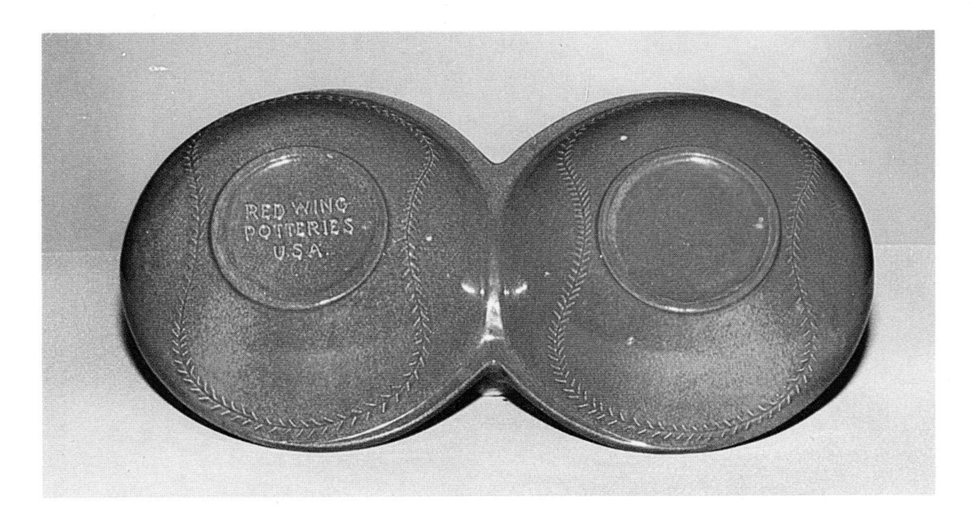

BOTTOM VIEW.

Wing

The wing ashtray produced by Red Wing was a very popular item. Many other companies purchased it with their advertising logo added. Shaped like the unmistakable red wing that was the pottery's trademark, it also was good advertising for Red Wing. Produced mostly in a heavy red glaze, it is occasionally found in another color, quite a find. These ashtrays are popular with collectors. Associated with the rare advertising and miniature pieces, they are a good find.

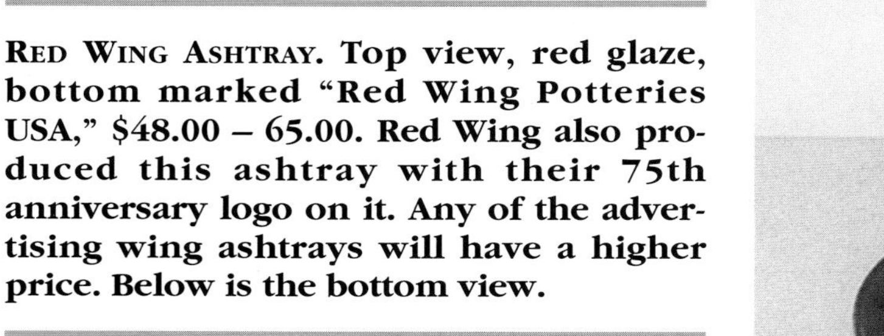

Red Wing Ashtray. Top view, red glaze, bottom marked "Red Wing Potteries USA," $48.00 – 65.00. Red Wing also produced this ashtray with their 75th anniversary logo on it. Any of the advertising wing ashtrays will have a higher price. Below is the bottom view.

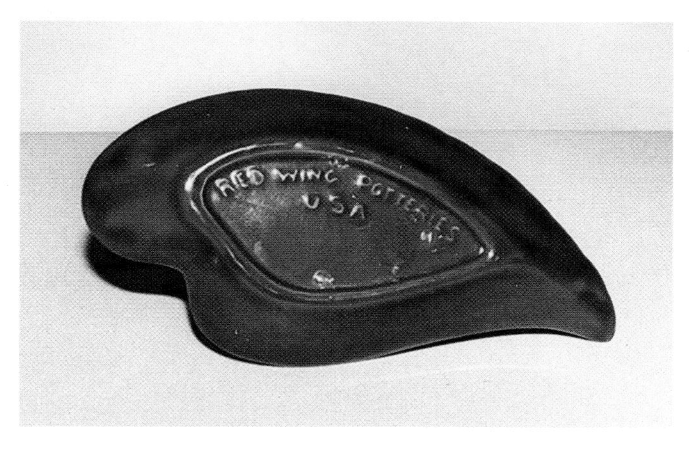

Bottom view.

Dinnerware

The dinnerware line of Red Wing Potteries was introduced in the mid 1930s with the Gypsy Trail line. Charles Murphy, an Ohio designer, was hired in 1940 to design dinnerware and art pottery. He created patterns with hand-painted designs for the Provincial line, introduced in 1941. These patterns were some of the most ornate and beautiful of the dinnerware lines. Eva Zeisel, a designer who had been with Red Wing for some years, created the Town & Country line in 1946.

Each of the dinnerware lines consisted of a full line of items including casseroles, coffee and water servers, teapots, salt and pepper shakers, and many accessory pieces. The lines were produced in a variety of different patterns and finishes, ranging from solid colors to hand-painted flowers, fruits, and other items. There were many different dinnerware lines and patterns produced over the years, some in more limited quantities than others. Patterns ranged from quite simple to quite ornate, requiring many brush strokes.

Some of the early pieces are not marked, but once you are familiar with the look of each pattern, you will be able to recognize them. The later lines were usually marked with a wing stamp and Red Wing. You will find some of these markings at the end of this book.

Red Wing continued to produce the dinnerware line until the close of the plant in 1967. A huge seller, the dinnerware line created a large place for Red Wing in the history of such ware. Many people collect Red Wing dinnerware. It makes both a beautiful and useful collection, for setting a beautiful table and for a lovely display in a china cabinet. The following pictures show that it would be a wonderful collection.

The dinnerware in this chapter, unless otherwise noted, is from the collection of Bev and Duane Brown. The Browns own and operate B & D Collectibles & Antiques, in Harlan, Iowa.

Gypsy Trail
(1935)

Gypsy Trail was the first line of dinnerware introduced by Red Wing in 1935. The line consisted of four patterns, Plain, Chevron, Reed, and Fondoso. All the patterns were produced in plain colors and included table settings along with many accessory pieces. Most pieces of this line are unmarked.

The following pictures are a sample of the Plain and Reed patterns. Due to the age of this line, the patterns are quite hard to find.

Reed Pattern

Produced in orange, yellow, ivory, royal blue, and turquoise, this pattern consisted of place settings, serving pieces, and many accessory items. Among them are pie plates, egg cups, pitchers, covered dishes, and candlesticks.

Reed Pattern Mixing Bowls. Unmarked, 5" – 10" set, gloss orange, yellow, and ivory, $95.00 – 135.00 set.

Plain Pattern

The plain pattern was originally produced in orange, yellow, royal blue, ivory, and turquoise; several pastel colors were added later. It also included many accessories, several different pitchers, a cookie jar, duck ashtray, and an oil cruet.

Plain Pattern Swirl Pitcher. Unmarked – 64 oz., gloss royal blue/white, pitcher $75.00 – 100.00. From the author's collection.

Provincial
(1941)

Introduced in 1941 the Provincial dinnerware was the first to be hand decorated. The line consisted of four patterns, Ardennes, Brittany, Normandy, and Orleans. Each pattern has a different hand-painted theme done in beautiful color. You should find the pieces in this line marked, with the exception of the salt and pepper shakers and perhaps the candleholders. Most of the salt and peppers produced by Red Wing were not marked, no matter what the vintage; this holds true with a lot of the candleholders also. The candleholders in this line are quite a find, but they are worth looking for because they will add a lot of beauty to your setting.

Brittany Pattern

The Brittany pattern featured a hand-painted yellow rose with a yellow band around the plate. This was the only color finish of the Brittany pattern. The accessory pieces were also hand painted and included serving pieces, salt and pepper, water jug, teapot, and candleholders.

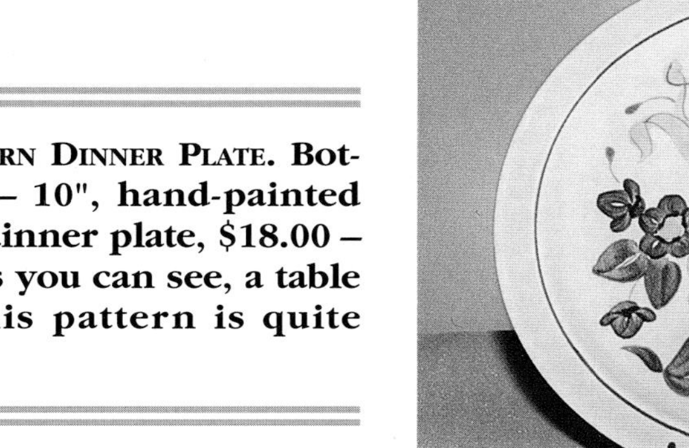

Brittany Pattern Dinner Plate. Bottom marked – 10", hand-painted yellow rose, dinner plate, $18.00 – 22.00 each. As you can see, a table setting in this pattern is quite lovely.

Orleans Pattern

The Orleans pattern featured a red rose and multi-colored other flowers, all hand painted. The accessories were also hand decorated and included the same pieces as the Brittany.

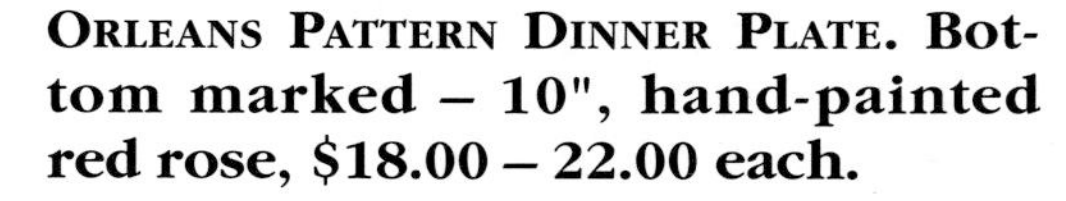

Orleans Pattern Dinner Plate. Bottom marked – 10", hand-painted red rose, $18.00 – 22.00 each.

Ardennes Pattern

The Ardennes pattern was hand decorated with a leaf border. The early pieces were white with the leaf band (pictured below); later the plates were white with the hand-painted leaf band placed on a light green outer border. The accessory pieces of this pattern were available in two colors, Dubonnet and forest green, and included the same items as the other patterns.

Ardennes Pattern Dinner Plate. Bottom marked – 10", hand-painted green leaves, $24.00 – 28.00 each. This is one of the early plates without the light green outer band.

Provincial Oomph
(1943)

Introduced in 1943, the Provincial Oomph line was a heavy utilitarian dinnerware, produced with a combination brown and aqua finish in place settings, serving pieces, and extensive pieces of bakeware. There were no other patterns in this line. Often confused with Village Green since the colors are similar, the Oomph has a smooth finish, while the Village Green is ribbed on the outside.

Provincial Oomph Dinner Plate. Bottom marked – 10", aqua/brown, dinner plate, $15.00 – 20.00 each. This plate is brown on the outside.

Provincial Oomph Mixing Bowls. Bottom marked – 6", 8" & 10" Bowls, brown/aqua, mixing bowls, $65.00 – 80.00 set. Notice this heavy look resembles the earlier stoneware. From the author's collection.

Concord
(1947)

The Concord line was introduced in 1947 and had the most patterns of any of the Red Wing dinnerware lines. There were 19 patterns, Blossom Time, Bud, Chrysanthemum, Fantasy, Fruit, Harvest, Iris, Leaf Magic, Lanterns, Lotus, Lexington, Magnolia, Morning Glory Pink, Morning Glory Blue, Nassau, Quartette, Spring Song, Willow Wind, and Zinnia. Too numerous to describe all in detail, some of the patterns featured the design on the accessory pieces, and others had solid colors on the outside. A number of these patterns make up some of the rare and very rare dinnerware items of today.

Below are eight of the patterns produced in the Concord line. Many of these patterns were hand-painted.

Morning Glory Pattern

Morning Glory was produced in two colors, pink and blue. The accessory pieces were finished in green, yellow, and gray. There were not as many accessory pieces in the Concord line. The following pictures show both colors available in the Morning Glory pattern.

Morning Glory Dinner Plate. Bottom marked – 10½", pink morning glory, dinner plate, $22.00 – 28.00 each.

Morning Glory Dinner Plate. Bottom marked – 10½", blue morning glory, dinner plate, $22.00 – 28.00 each.

Willow Wind Pattern

The Willow Wind pattern was finished with pink and gray leaves on a white background. The accessory pieces match the plates. All the patterns in the Concord line have the same shape.

Willow Wind Dinner Plate. Bottom marked – 10½", gray and pink leaves, $26.00 – 30.00 each.

Lotus Pattern

The Lotus pattern was designed with a white lotus blossom accented with bronze-metallic, green and brown, hand-painted on the items. The accessories were available in bronze-metallic, chartreuse, and gray. This was a very popular pattern in the Red Wing dinnerware line.

Lotus Dinner Plate. Bottom marked – 10½", hand-painted, white lotus blossom, dinner plate, $20.00 – 24.00 each. Most of the Red Wing dinnerware that was hand-painted is marked as such on the bottom.

Nassau Pattern

This pattern in decorated with green, brown, and yellow leaves and flowers. Not often found, this is one of the rare Red Wing dinnerware patterns.

Nassau Dinner Plate. Bottom marked – 10½", green, yellow, and brown leaves, rare dinner plate, $80.00 – 100.00 each. This pattern has been known to sell for over $125.00 per plate.

Harvest Pattern

The Harvest Pattern features multi-colored fruit on a white background with a yellow rim. The accessories are decorated the same. This is a very rare pattern and extremely hard to find. Quite attractive, it makes a lovely table setting.

Harvest Dinner Plate. Bottom marked – 10½", multi-colored fruit, very rare dinner plate, $85.00 – 125.00 each. These Harvest plates have sold for over $150.00 each.

Blossom Time Pattern

This pattern was decorated with a red rose on a white background. The accessory pieces were produced in yellow and green. As you can see, all the patterns in the Concord line were very pretty.

Blossom Time Dinner Plate. Bottom marked – 10½", red rose, dinner plate, $20.00 – 26.00 each. As you may have noticed, all the patterns in the Concord Line have the same shape.

Zinnia Pattern

The Zinnia pattern was decorated with a yellow zinnia and light green lupine leaves on a white background. The accessory pieces were available in gray, copper, yellow, and green.

Zinnia Dinner Plate. Bottom marked – 10½", yellow zinnia, dinner plate, $22.00 – 26.00 each.

Iris Pattern

Iris was produced with multi-colored flowers and leaves on a white background. The accessory pieces came in mulberry.

IRIS PLACE SETTING, Sugar Bowl, and Spoon Rest. Bottom marked – 10½", multi-colored, Iris dinner plate, $30.00 – 35.00 each, Iris cup & saucer, $25.00 – 30.00 set, Iris sugar bowl, $25.00 – 30.00 each with lid, Iris spoon rest, $40.00 – 50.00 each. These spoon rests are hard to find, but add a finishing touch to a dinnerware collection.

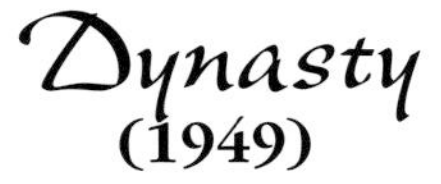

Dynasty (1949)

There was only one pattern, Plum Blossom, produced in the Dynasty line. Produced in two colors of finish, pink and yellow on a white background on a full line of dinnerware, the accessories came in a choice of chartreuse, forest green, and metallic brown.

DYNASTY DINNER PLATE. Bottom marked – 10½", hand-painted, yellow blossoms, dinner plate, $18.00 – 24.00 each. The pink finish is identical to the yellow except for color.

Village Green
(1953)

Introduced in 1953, Village Green was the second most popular line of Red Wing dinnerware. Its sales spanned a decade. This was a complete line including a 2-gallon water cooler. Glazed in brown and aqua, Village Green was a heavy utilitarian dinnerware.

Although not as ornate as some of the other dinnerware, a set of Village Green would make a very nice collection. Pieces from this line can be found quite often.

Village Green Water Cooler With Stand & Beverage Mugs. Unmarked – 2-gallon water cooler, beverage mugs, gloss brown/aqua, water cooler, $525.00 – 675.00 with stand, mugs, $20.00 – 30.00 each. The water coolers with stands are very hard to find and the pricing will reflect that.

Anniversary
(1953)

Introduced in 1953, this line received its name because that year was Red Wing's 75th anniversary. There were six patterns in this line, Capistrano, Country Garden, Driftwood, Midnight Rose, Pink Spice, and Tweed Tex, produced in a full line of dinnerware with several colors available for the accessories. The accessories colors could be used with all the patterns. Many of the accessory pieces in this line had a basket weave texture. Any of these Anniversary patterns would make a lovely collection.

Midnight Rose Pattern

The Midnight Rose pattern was finished with a black and gray rose on a white background. The accessories were available in black. This has a very striking finish and is also one of the very rare Red Wing dinnerware patterns.

Midnight Rose Dinner Plate. Bottom marked – 10½", gray and black rose, very rare dinner plate, $145.00 – 175.00 each.

Capistrano Pattern

The Capistrano pattern was hand-painted with a yellow-breasted black bird and colored foliage on a white background. The design was sealed under the glaze in order to prevent fading. The accessory pieces were a soft sage green with the basket-weave texture.

Capistrano Dinner Plate. Bottom marked – 10½", yellow and black bird, dinner plate, $22.00 – 26.00 each.

TWEED TEX PATTERN

The Tweed Tex pattern had no decoration added. It was a plain white color with basket weave texture. Any color accessory could be used with this pattern.

TWEED TEX DINNER PLATE. Bottom marked – 10½", white basket weave, dinner plate, $15.00 – 18.00 each.

COUNTRY GARDEN PATTERN

Country Garden has flowers and leaves of blue, greens, lavender, and pink on a white background. The accessory pieces were offered in gray basket weave. One of the more decorated patterns, it is quite lovely.

COUNTRY GARDEN DINNER PLATE. Bottom marked 10½", multi-colored, dinner plate, $35.00 – 45.00 each.

DRIFTWOOD PATTERN

The Driftwood pattern was decorated with blue flowers on brown driftwood. The accessories are blue. This is a simple but elegant pattern.

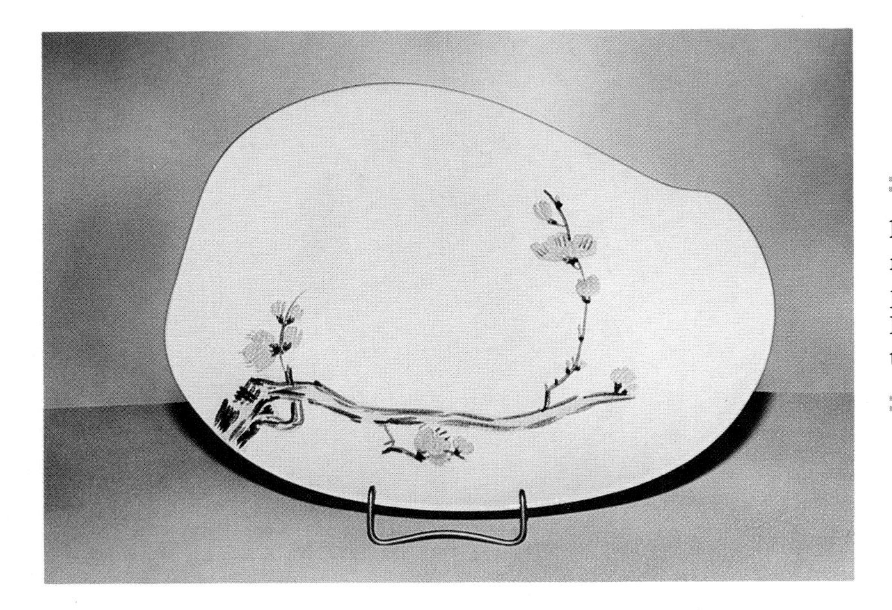

DRIFTWOOD PLATTER. Bottom marked – 15", blue flowered, platter, $36.00 – 40.00 each. Notice the contoured shape of this platter.

PINK SPICE PATTERN

Pink Spice is hand-painted with flowers in shades of pink and a yellow butterfly. The accessory pieces are lavender, and were later produced in pink. This is another very lovely pattern.

PINK SPICE BUFFET BOWL. Bottom marked – 10½", pink flowered, buffet bowl, $46.00 – 54.00 each.

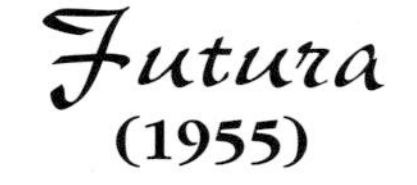

Futura
(1955)

First produced in 1955, there are 10 patterns in the Futura line, Crazy Rhythm, Colonnes, Frontenac, Golden Viking, Lupine, Montmartre, Northern Lights, Random Harvest, Red Wing Rose, and Tampico. A full line of dinnerware, the accessories included pitchers, a teapot and cover, a five-compartment nut bowl, and a trivet. The trivets of any line a quite hard to find, but add value to your collection. The Tampico pattern also included a two-gallon water cooler with stand. Any of the trivets are very rare.

Below are six of the 10 patterns in the Futura line. There is also a picture of the Tampico water cooler with stand.

Tampico Pattern

The Tampico pattern is hand-painted in greens and browns with a melon accent on a brown flecked background. The accessories match the dinnerware.

Tampico Place Setting. Bottom marked – 10½" plate, green, brown, and melon, dinner plate, $28.00 – 35.00 each, cup & saucer, $30.00 – 38.00 set. The Tampico pattern is very popular among collectors and the pricing is considerably higher than the other patterns.

Tampico Water Coolers With Stands. Two-gallon cooler, greens, browns, with melon accent, $525.00 – 700.00 each, with stand. This is a magnificent collection of the Tampico water coolers. Any of the water coolers with stands are very hard to find.

Montmartre Pattern

This pattern is hand-painted in browns and yellow on a white background. The picture gives an international flavor to this pattern. The accessory pieces match the dinnerware pattern.

Montmartre Dinner Plate. Bottom marked – 10½", browns and yellow, dinner plate, $35.00 – 45.00 each.

Golden Viking Pattern

The Golden Viking pattern is hand-painted in a gold and brown leaf pattern which covers the entire plate. The accessory pieces are covered in the same design. A Danish design, this pattern has the look of an every day dinnerware.

Golden Viking Dinner Plate. Bottom marked – 10½", gold and brown, dinner plate, $18.00 – 22.00 each. The Northern Lights pattern, which is not pictured, is identical to this except done in turquoise.

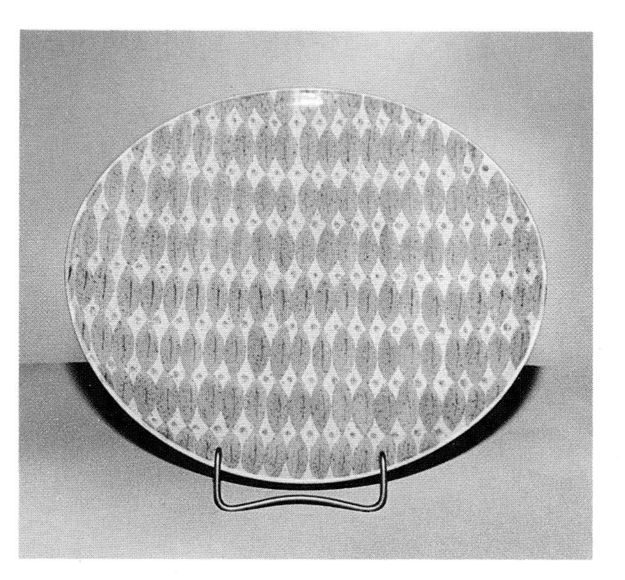

Crazy Rhythm Pattern

The Crazy Rhythm pattern is done is browns and gold on a tan fleck background. The pattern is very modern looking. The accessories match the dinnerware. This pattern was very popular for every day use.

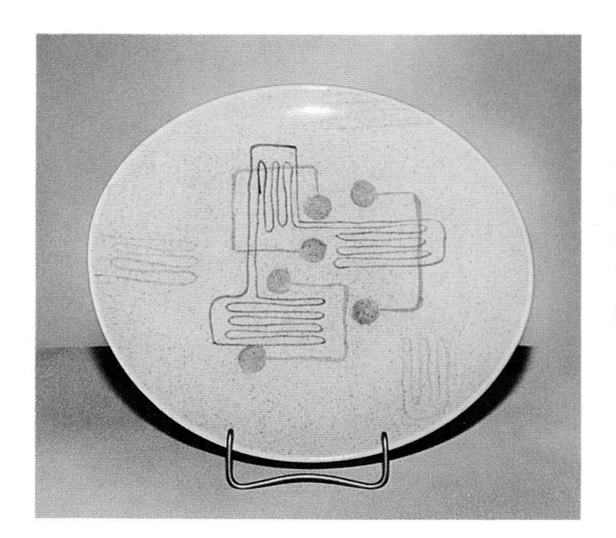

Crazy Rhythm Dinner Plate. Bottom marked – 10½", browns and gold, dinner plate, $18.00 – 22.00 each.

Random Harvest Pattern

This pattern has hand-painted leaves and flowers in rich browns, greens, and copper. Accented with turquoise and coral on a brown fleck background, the accessory pieces are also done in this pattern.

Random Harvest Place Setting. Bottom marked – 10½" plate, multi-colored, dinner plate $22.00 – 28.00 each, cup & saucer $15.00 – 18.00 set.

Random Harvest Accessories. Most bottom marked, front clockwise; sugar with cover $25.00 – 30.00, casserole with cover $36.00 – 40.00, relish tray $26.00 – 34.00, two quart water pitcher $40.00 – 48.00, gravy boat $25.00 – 30.00, creamer $22.00 – 26.00. All pricing is per piece.

Red Wing Rose Pattern

The Red Wing Rose pattern was finished with a pink rose with brown leaves on a white background. The accessories matched the dinnerware design.

Red Wing Rose Relish Dish. Bottom marked, pink and brown, relish dish, $20.00 – 28.00 each.

Casual
(1955)

The Casual line was first introduced in 1955 with the Smart Set. There were four other patterns, each introduced after 1955. They were Bob White, Hearthside, Round Up, and Tip Toe. A complete line, Casual has a wide variety of accessories. There were multiple casseroles with warmer stands, a teapot with warmer, beverage servers with stands, and a lazy Susan with carrier. Bob White and Round Up also came with two-gallon water coolers with stands. A complete set of any of these patterns would be a magnificent collection.

Following are four of the five patterns in the Casual line.

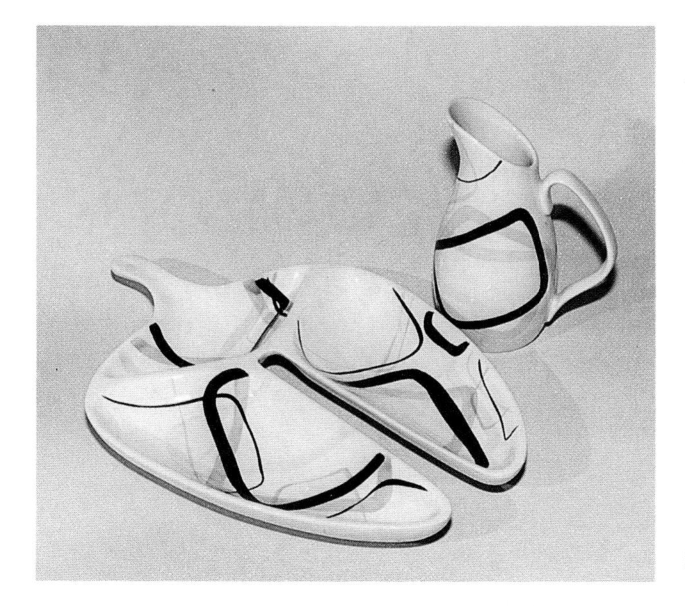

Smart Set Pattern

Introduced in 1955, this was a popular set for Red Wing, finished in black, gold, and gray geometric designs on a white background. All accessories matched the dinnerware.

Smart Set Accessories. Bottom marked, black, gold, and gray design, compartment relish tray, $28.00 – 35.00 each, creamer $18.00 – 26.00 each.

Bob White Pattern

Introduced in 1956, the Bob White pattern was the most popular of the Red Wing dinnerware and was hand-painted in browns and turquoise with a bob white bird in foliage on a brown flecked background. The many accessory pieces matched the dinnerware and included a pepper mill (which is very rare), a cookie jar, and hors d'oeuvre holder. Many of these pieces are hard to find, and a complete set would be a very valuable collection.

Bob White Accessories. Most bottom marked, Bob White design, center front clockwise; bird salt & pepper $42.00 – 48.00 set, tall salt and pepper $40.00 – 45.00 set, cookie jar $125.00 – 175.00 with cover, two-gallon water cooler with stand $625.00 – 775.00, two-quart casserole with cover and stand $60.00 – 75.00, hors d'oeuvre holder $50.00 – 60.00. Bob White is the only pattern that has the hors d'oeuvre holder.

Tip Toe Pattern

Tip Toe was introduced in 1958 and was finished with gold and brown tulips on a white background with a tan border. The accessories matched the dinnerware.

Tip Toe Dinner Plate. Bottom marked – 10½", gold and brown tulips, dinner plate, $10.00 – 15.00.

Round Up Pattern

The Round Up pattern introduced in 1958 has a multi-colored Western motif on a tan fleck background. There are two different Western designs of this pattern. The accessories have the same design as the dinnerware. Round Up is very popular among collectors and is very hard to find. You will also notice the pricing is considerably higher than most dinnerware.

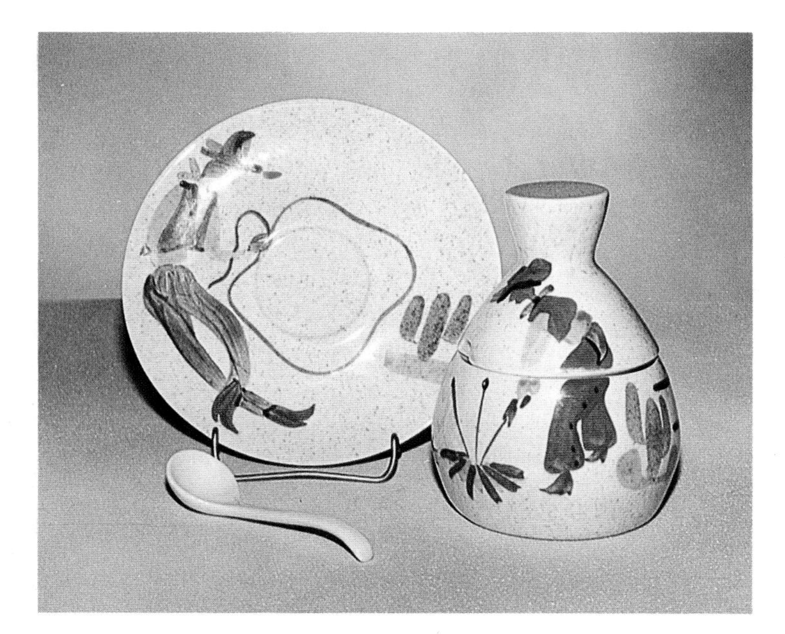

Round Up Saucer & Sugar Bowl. Western motif, saucer $25.00 – 30.00 each, sugar bowl with cover $52.00 – 65.00 each.

Contemporary
(1956)

Introduced in 1956, the Contemporary line included the White & Turquoise pattern and the Spruce pattern. Both were advertised for kitchen, oven, and table.

Spruce Pattern

Finished in blues, white, and brown, the Spruce pattern has the look of dinnerware produced for everyday use. It included the usual table pieces along with casseroles, bean pots, pitchers, a salad bowl, and canister jars.

Spruce Dinner Plate. Bottom marked – 10½", blue and white, dinner plate, $30.00 – 38.00 each. The pricing on this pattern is higher than most of the plainer patterns.

White & Turquoise Pattern

The White & Turquoise pattern consisted of the same accessory pieces as Spruce. It was advertised for kitchen, table, and oven, but it is believed that the table setting pieces were made in limited quantity. Therefore, the place settings are very hard, if not impossible, to find. Finished in turquoise and black on a white background, this pattern definitely has a contemporary look.

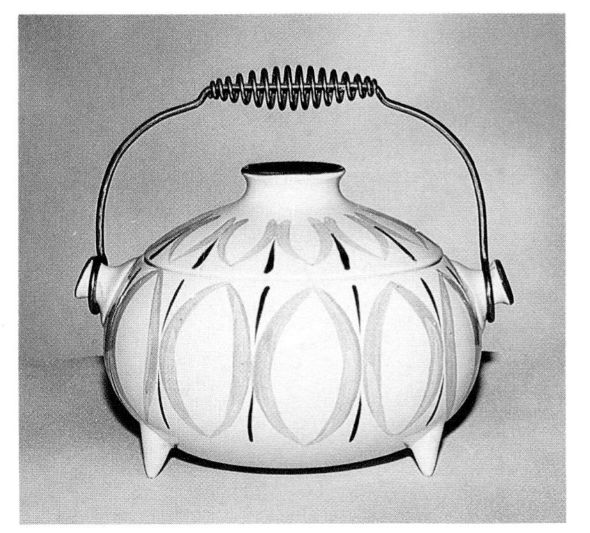

White & Turquoise Bean Pot. Two-quart, white & turquoise, bean pot, $42.00 – 48.00 with cover and handle.

Two Step
(1960)

Two Step was not advertised as a pattern, rather as dinnerware itself. Finished in brown and turquoise on a tan flecked background, Two Step was a full line dinnerware. Besides table setting pieces, it included pitchers, platters, and many serving pieces with warmers.

Two Step Dinner Plate, Bowl, Salt & Pepper. Bottom marked, brown & turquoise, dinner plate – 10½" $22.00 – 28.00 each, bowl $8.00 – 12.00 each, salt & pepper $18.00 – 25.00 set.

(1960)

Introduced in 1960, the True China line was made with china clay instead of the coarser pottery clay Red Wing had used until this point. There are eight patterns in this line, Crocus, Daisy Chain, Granada, Lute Song, Majestic, Mediterrania, Merrileaf, and Vintage. All the patterns were hand painted and carried a one-year warranty against breakage. The patterns included table-setting pieces, along with serving pieces.

Lute Song Pattern

Lute Song was finished with turquoise and brown instruments on a tan fleck background. The accessory pieces matched the dinnerware.

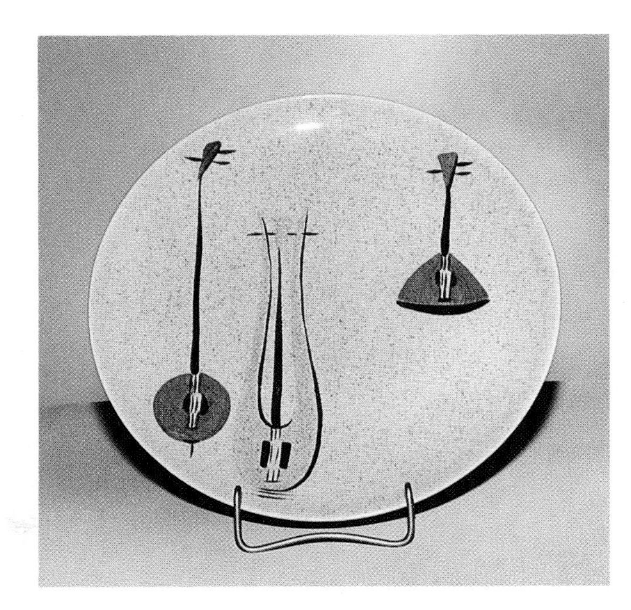

Lute Song Dinner Plate. Bottom marked – 10", brown and turquoise, dinner plate, $25.00 – 30.00 each.

Mediterrania Pattern

Mediterrania is floral on a white background, finished in blues and greens. Like other patterns in this line, the hand-painted designs were soft and very lovely.

Mediterrania Dinner Plate. Bottom marked – 10", blue and green, dinner plate, $28.00 – 32.00 each.

Daisy Chain Pattern

This pattern was finished in gray daisies accented with rust, brown, chartreuse, and green. In all the patterns, the hand-painted finish was sealed beneath the glaze which kept it from fading.

Daisy Chain Dinner Plate. Bottom marked – 10", multi-color daisy chain, dinner plate, $30.00 – 38.00 each.

Merrileaf Pattern

The Merrileaf pattern is finished in aqua and tan, hand-painted in soft tones. The accessories match the table setting.

Merrileaf Dinner Plate. Bottom marked – 10", aqua and tan, dinner plate, $25.00 – 30.00 each.

VINTAGE PATTERN

The Vintage pattern is hand-painted in soft grays and orchid with grapes and leaves on a white background. The design is very pale, as shown in the following picture. The accessories match the table setting.

VINTAGE DINNER PLATE. Bottom marked – 10", gray and orchid grape, dinner plate, $24.00 – 30.00 each.

Cylinder
(1962)

Introduced in 1962, Cylinder has six patterns, Desert Sun, Flight, Pepe, Pompeii, Tahitian Gold, and Turtle Dove. These patterns were all full lines including serving dishes, casserole, pitcher, teapot, bean pot, and an ashtray. The Flight pattern is one of the rare dinnerware collectibles of today. It is very hard to find and quite expensive.

Desert Sun Pattern

Desert Sun was hand-painted in orange, gray, and brown in a sunburst around the edge on a white background. The serving pieces are tan with the orange and brown covers.

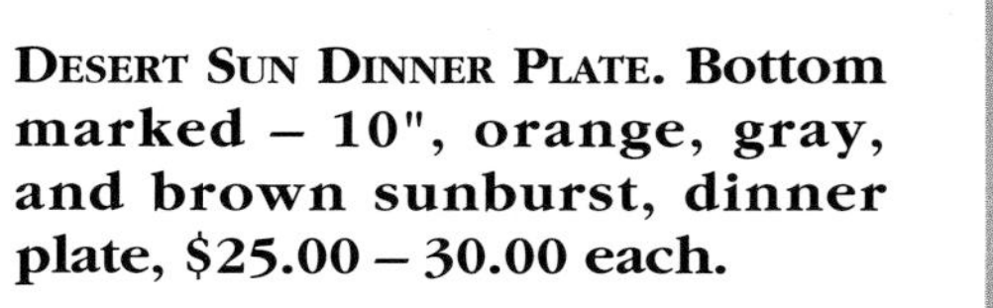

Desert Sun Dinner Plate. Bottom marked – 10", orange, gray, and brown sunburst, dinner plate, $25.00 – 30.00 each.

Turtle Dove Pattern

Turtle Dove is hand-painted with browns and yellow turtledoves on a tan fleck background. The accessory pieces are tan fleck topped in yellow.

Turtle Dove Dinner Plate. Bottom marked – 10", brown and yellow turtledoves, dinner plate, $15.00 – 20.00 each.

Pepe Pattern

Pepe was finished with an orange and mauve Spanish accent on a tan fleck background. The accessories match the tableware.

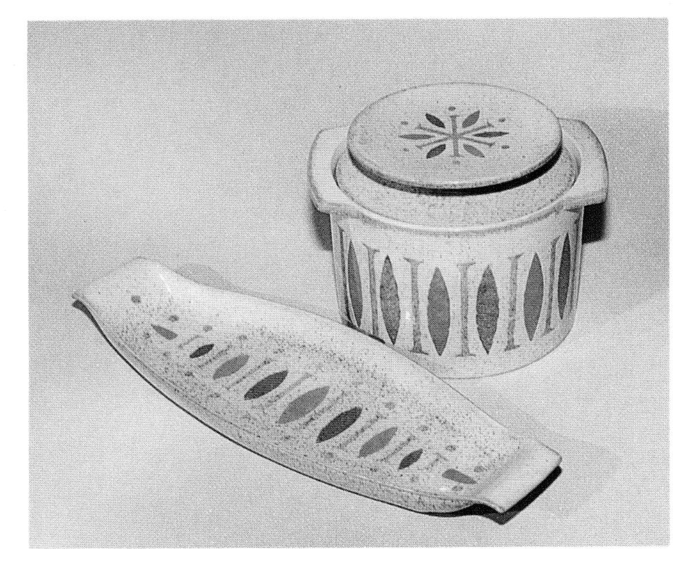

Pepe Bread Tray & Bean Pot. Bottom marked, orange and mauve Spanish motif, Bread Tray $30.00 – 38.00 each, Bean Pot $32.00 – 40.00 with cover.

Flight Pattern

The Flight pattern is finished with black, brown, and beige birds in flight on a white background. The accessories are tan with rust and brown covers. This pattern is very popular and it is also quite rare. You will have to look for quite awhile to find any of this pattern, and you can expect to pay high prices.

Flight Place Setting. Bottom marked – 10", birds in flight, rare dinner plate $100.00 – 135.00 each, rare cup & saucer $55.00 – 70.00 set.

FLIGHT DIVIDED VEGETABLE DISH. Bottom marked, birds in flight, rare vegetable dish, $60.00 – 75.00 each.

Provincial
(1963)

The Provincial line was first introduced during World War II as a bakeware line. It was reintroduced in 1963 with the addition of the tableware. The tableware is finished in a bittersweet red glaze. The accessories have a tan stone-like finish with bittersweet red glaze on the inside and the lids. They include a bean pot and casserole in several sizes.

PROVINCIAL PLACE SETTING. Bottom marked – 10", bittersweet red, dinner plate $12.00 – 18.00 each, cup & saucer $8.00 – 12.00 set.

Like True China
(1964)

Produced in almost the same shape as its counterpart True China, Like True China differs in that it was made from potter's clay rather than china clay. There are four patterns in this line, Blue Shadows, Brocade, Damask, and Kashmir. A full line of dinnerware, it includes table-setting pieces along with accessories such as a bread tray, teapot, beverage server and an ashtray.

Kashmir Pattern

Kashmir has a brown design on a rust background. This pattern has a different design than the other three.

Kashmir Dinner Plate. Bottom marked – 10½", brown design, dinner plate, $18.00 – 25.00 each.

Brocade Pattern

The Brocade Pattern has a gold design on a blue background. This design is the same on both the Blue Shadows and Damask patterns. Blue Shadows is blue on a light blue background and Damask is brown on a light brown background.

Brocade Dinner Plate. Bottom marked – 10½", gold design, dinner plate, $20.00 – 28.00 each.

(1965)

Ebb Tide was less ornate than most of the Red Wing dinnerware. It was finished with a dark green swirl on a green background. There are not as many accessories as some of the other dinnerware lines. They were finished the same, and included serving dishes such as platters, salad bowl, and casserole.

Ebb Tide Place Setting. Bottom marked – 10", green swirl, dinner plate $18.00 – 24.00 each, cup & saucer $10.00 – 15.00 set.

Ceramastone
(1967)

Ceramastone was one of the last dinnerware lines that Red Wing produced before the plant closed in 1967. The dinnerware was made from stoneware clay and included six patterns, Adobestone, Charstone Bleu, Greenwichstone, Heatherstone, Hearthstone Orange, and Hearthstone Beige. The accessories matched and included casseroles, a teapot, canisters, and candleholders.

HEARTHSTONE ORANGE DINNER PLATE. Bottom marked – 10", orange, dinner plate, $12.00 – 18.00 each.

HEARTHSTONE ORANGE SINGLE CANDLEHOLDER. No bottom mark, orange, candleholder, $55.00 – 75.00. A large candle is placed on the flat top. The candleholders from any of the dinnerware lines are hard to find and are higher priced. You will find that any of the Red Wing novelty items are expensive when you can find them. From author's collection.

Dinnerware Ashtrays

Three ashtrays from the Red Wing dinnerware lines are shown below. The duck ashtrays are from the Gypsy Trail, plain pattern. The other one is from the True China line and was the same in the Like True China. Ashtrays from the dinnerware lines are very hard to find and quite high in price. However, if you persist and are able to find the one that matches your pattern, it is worthwhile.

DINNERWARE ASHTRAYS. No bottom marks, orange and aqua duck ashtrays $30.00 – 45.00 each, tan fleck ashtray $22.00 – 30.00 each.

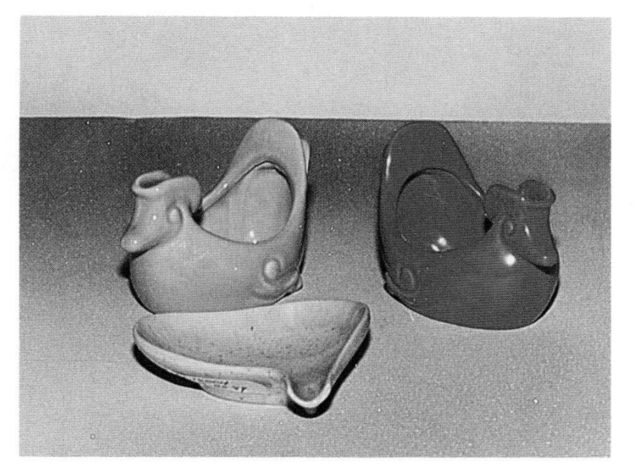

Salt & Pepper Shakers

The following pictures are a look at some of the many salt and pepper shakers that came with the dinnerware patterns. These have been grouped together, but will give you a good idea of what to look for. It is not easy to find a certain pattern, but it can be done. Most of the salt and pepper shakers are not marked, but can be identified by the finish design.

DINNERWARE SALT & PEPPER SHAKERS. No bottom marks, all are priced per set, outside circle clockwise from center front; Bob White Birds $40.00 – 50.00, Tampico $20.00 – 25.00, Brocade $18.00 – 22.00, Merrileaf $18.00 – 22.00, Lute Song $20.00 – 25.00, Random Harvest $20.00 – 25.00, Anniversary $18.00 – 22.00, center clockwise; Golden Viking $15.00 – 20.00, Pepe $15.00 – 20.00, Cylinder miscellaneous $10.00 – 15.00. This last set was meant to sell with a tall and short shaker like the Pepe. However, some people chose to purchase the two short pieces. They probably liked the look better.

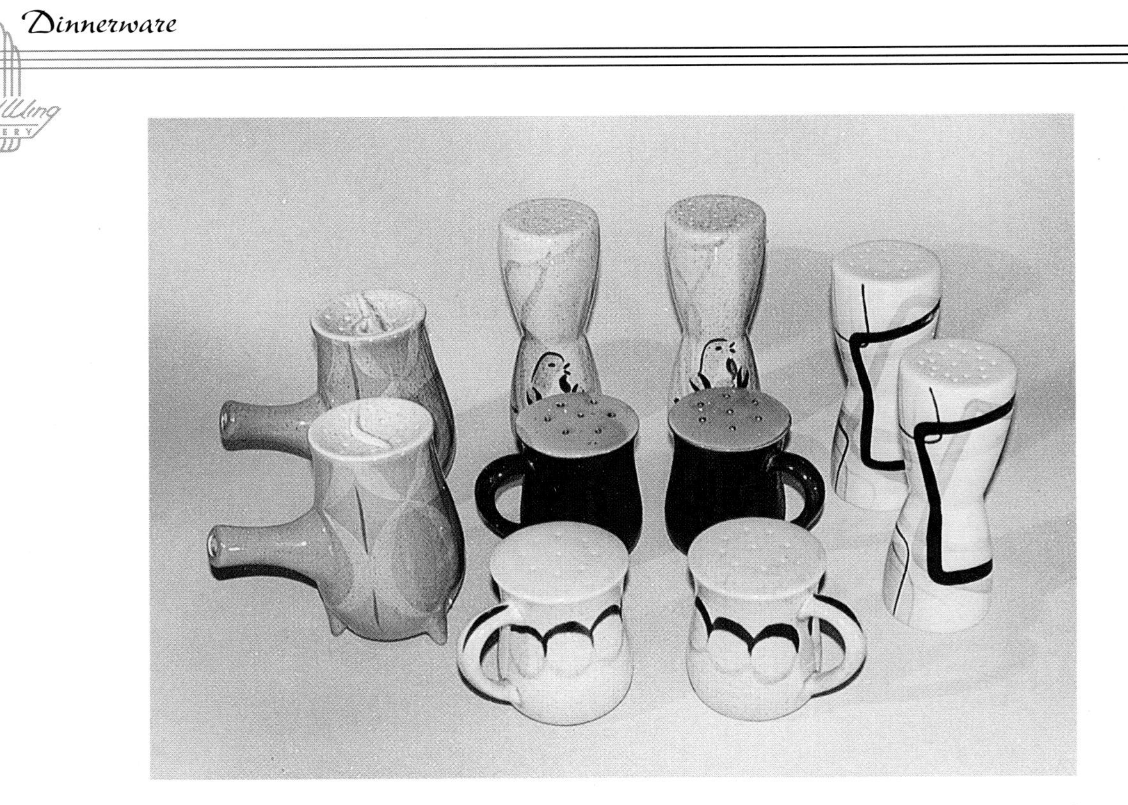

Dinnerware Salt & Pepper Shakers. No bottom marks, all are priced per set, center front clockwise; Two Step $20.00 – 25.00, Spruce $38.00 – 45.00, Bob White Tall $40.00 – 45.00, Smart Set 40.00 – 45.00, center; Village Green $30.00 – 35.00.

Dinnerware Salt & Pepper Shakers. No bottom marks, all are priced per set, front left to right; Iris $20.00 – 25.00, Blossom Time $20.00 – 25.00, Zinnia $20.00 – 25.00, Provincial Oomph $18.00 – 22.00, Gypsy Trail Plain $20.00 – 25.00, Brittany $20.00 – 25.00.

Miscellaneous

The following pictures are of miscellaneous items produced by Red Wing that fit into the dinnerware category.

JUICER. #256, yellow juicer, $140.00 – 165.00. This juicer also has a small glass to fit under the spout. Although rarely found it would increase the pricing quite a lot to have the set. This price is for juicer only.

HAMM'S MUG. Brown, Hamm's beer mug, $60.00 – 80.00 each. Print on mug reads Hamm's Krug Klub.

Cake Carrier. Bottom marked "One Of A Kind," dark green, embossed cake carrier, $150.00 – 225.00 complete as shown. This is an unusual item. It is said that this cake carrier was made for a person connected with Red Wing dinnerware. It is very hard to price one-of-a-kind pieces; the pricing given could vary considerably.

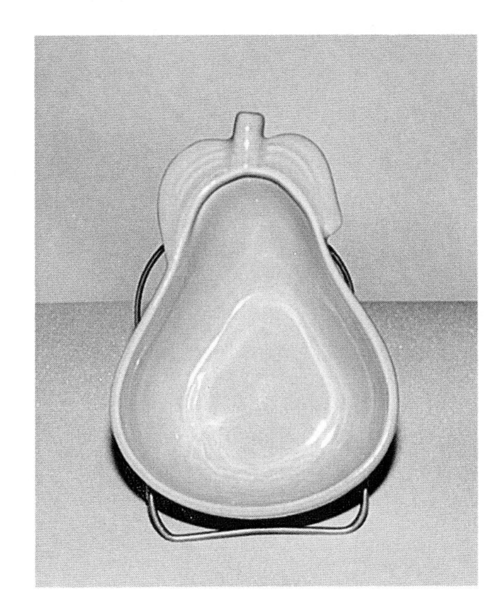

Marmalade Dish. Bottom marked – 4½", aqua, pear-shaped marmalade dish, $15.00 – 20.00 each. These dishes also came in a larger size with a lid. From author's collection.

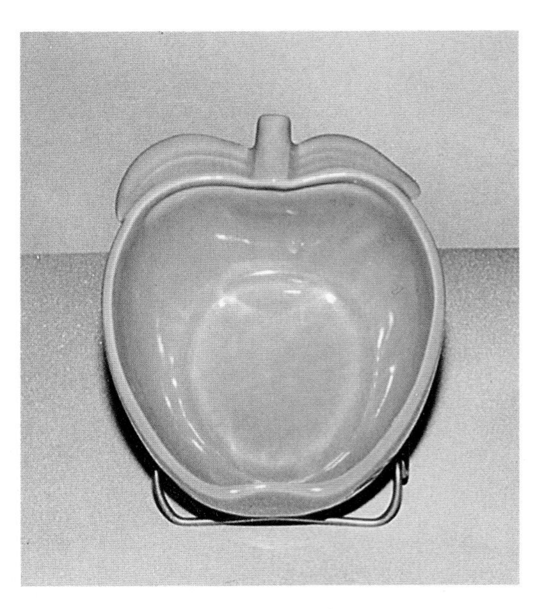

Marmalade Dish. Bottom marked – 4½", coral, apple-shaped marmalade dish, $15.00 – 20.00 each. From author's collection.

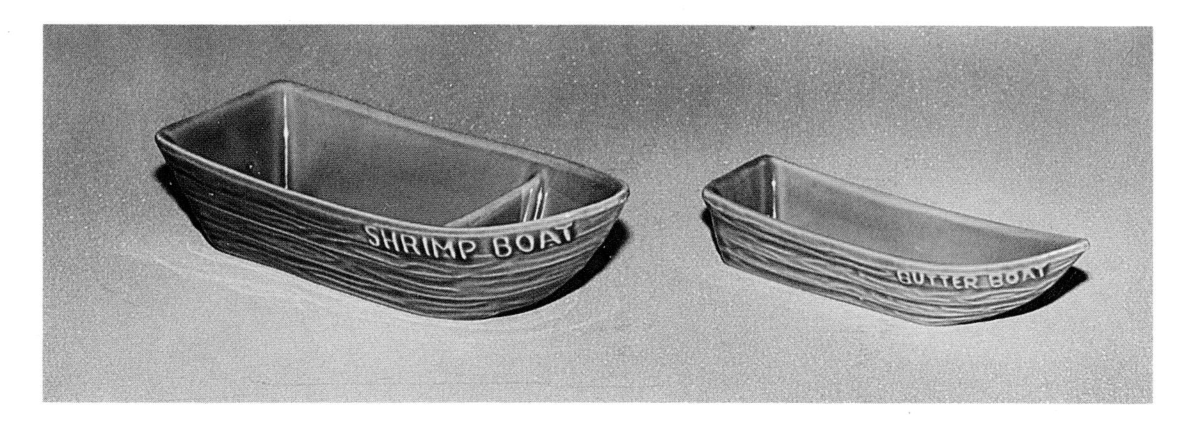

Novelty Boat Dishes. No bottom marks, light brown, boat dishes, shrimp boat $12.00 – 18.00 each, butter boat $10.00 – 15.00 each. It is said there is another larger boat to this set, perhaps labeled dream boat.

Teapots. #257 & 260, Bottom marked, Red Wing teapots, #257 – Yellow Chicken teapot, $115.00 – 130.00 each. #260 – Pink Lady teapot $120.00 – 135.00 each.

Cookie Jars

Red Wing produced several varieties of cookie jars over the years. Some matched dinnerware sets and others were novelty creations. Below is a sample of some of the jars produced. Earlier in the chapter with the Bob White grouping an example of the jars made to match the dinnerware was shown. Not all the cookie jars are bottom marked; some have the dinnerware stamp and others no marking at all. You will eventually be able to tell that the unmarked jars are Red Wing by the style. Pricing on these jars assumes that they are in very good condition.

Red Wing Cookie Jar. Bottom marked, yellow and brown, Friar Tuck cookie jar, $110.00 – 140.00. From author's collection.

Red Wing Cookie Jar. No bottom marks, multi-colored peasant, cookie jar, $85.00 – 110.00. From the author's collection. Large serving bowls to match this cookie jar were also made.

Red Wing Cookie Jar. Bottom marked, red flowered, saffron cookie jar, $165.00 – 195.00. Notice this cookie jar has the look of stoneware.

Red Wing Cookie Jar. No bottom mark, tan fleck, Happy cookie jar, $175.00 – 225.00. This cookie jar was named "Happy" because of the verse on the front. It reads "Happy the children, wherever they are, who live in a house, with a full cookie jar.

Red Wing Cookie Jar. No bottom mark, yellow, barrel cookie jar, $85.00 – 115.00.

Bottom Markings

Most of the Red Wing Pottery is marked in some manner on the bottom of the piece. There are some exceptions in each category; one example is the candleholders, very few of which have any bottom markings. You will also find some brushed ware pieces with no markings and some of the cookie jars. The reason for this is unclear. Perhaps the pieces were missed or maybe workers chose not to mark certain items. However, most of the Red Wing art ware you find will indicate on the bottom that it is indeed Red Wing.

Later, numbers were added to the bottom markings. These numbers were Red Wing's production numbers, called shape numbers. They were also used as catalog numbers for items. These numbers stayed the same through all the years of production of a specific piece. As mentioned earlier, some of the shapes were produced from the 1930s until 1967 when the plant closed. Letters sometimes preceded the shape number; these were an indication of the artist who designed that certain piece of art pottery.

The following pictures will give an overview of some of these bottom markings.

Brushed Ware Markings

The Brushed Ware line has an ink stamp marking, usually done in blue. You will also find that most of this early line has no colored glaze on the bottom of the piece.

Brushed Ware Bottom Stamp. Bottom marking on a brushed ware vase. This is the most common marking you will see on Brushed Ware.

Brushed Ware Bottom Stamp. Bottom marking on a brushed ware vase. You will also find this smaller ink stamp with no circle on the brushed ware. The stamp reads "RED WING ART POTTERY."

Glazed Ware Markings

The early Glazed Ware (late 1920s to early 1930s) was bottom stamped the same as the last ink stamp shown on previous pages. This early art ware also was not color glazed on the bottom, having the rough appearance of the Brushed Ware on the bottom.

Later in the 1930s Red Wing started inscribing by hand RED WING and the shape number on the bottom of the art ware before it was fired. They later also added the inscription U.S.A. to the markings. The exception to this is RumRill which was marked as such. Eventually Red Wing stamped these inscriptions on the art ware also.

Some of the glazed ware you will find has a letter preceding the shape number. This letter indicates the artist who designed the piece, e.g., a B for Belle Kogan, M for Charles Murphy.

The following pictures will give you an example of each of these markings, including RumRill. Some of the early glazed ware will have the RED WING ART POTTERY ink stamp that was used on the Brushed Ware.

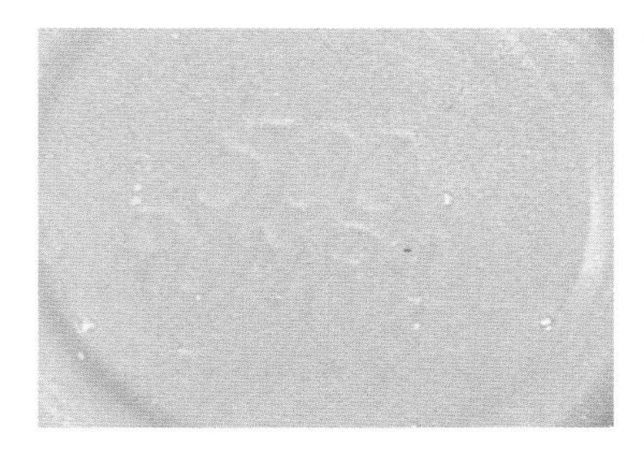

RumRill Bottom Marking. 500 above RUMRILL.

RumRill Bottom Marking. 315 above RumRill.

Glazed Ware Bottom Marking, with letter.

Glazed Ware Bottom Marking, complete with U.S.A.

Early Glazed Ware Bottom Marking, without the U.S.A.

Glazed Ware Bottom Marking, complete.

GLAZED WARE BOTTOM MARKING, ornate S.

GLAZED WARE BOTTOM MARKING with letter.

GLAZED WARE BOTTOM MARKING with size.

DINNERWARE MARKINGS

There is quite a variety of bottom markings on Red Wing dinnerware. Many include a wing stamp of some sort. One such wing stamp is identical to one of the wing labels added on some of the glazed ware. Other pieces have a stamp with writing explaining the specifics of the line. For instance, the saffron ware is stamped RED WING SAFFRON WARE.

Below are examples of some of the marking you will find on the dinnerware lines.

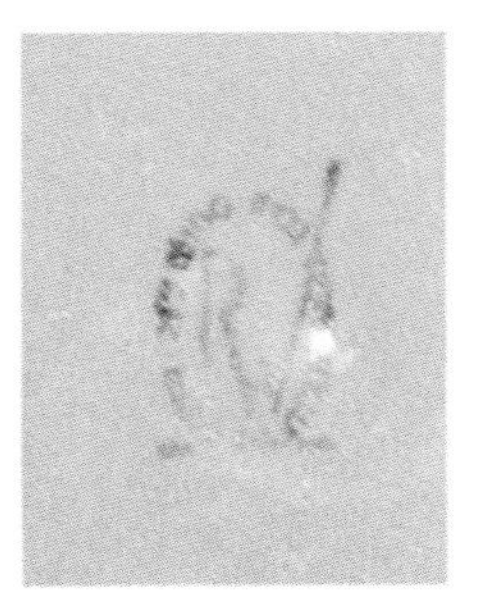

DINNERWARE BOTTOM MARKING. RED WING POTTERY HAND PAINTED with the initials RW inside the circle.

DINNERWARE BOTTOM MARKING. Red Wing Pottery, HAND PAINTED

DINNERWARE BOTTOM MARKING.

DINNERWARE BOTTOM MARKING.

MISCELLANEOUS DINNERWARE BOTTOM MARKING.

MISCELLANEOUS DINNERWARE BOTTOM MARKINGS.

Wing Labels

Some of the Red Wing Art Pottery you find will have a paper wing label glued somewhere on the piece. It is not known what the selection method was for doing this, but articles that are found with the label intact are worth from $5.00 to $15.00 more in value, depending on the item and the condition of the label. The labels were placed randomly on the pieces of pottery. Some were even placed sideways. The wing labels came in gold or silver with a red wing and red lettering. There is also a smaller, perhaps earlier version that is red with silver markings on it. Some special edition labels have also been found. One such label is like the gold with red wing except it includes writing marking the 75th anniversary of Red Wing. Following are examples of some of the labels you will find.

RED WING LABEL. Probably the first label used in the 1930s.

GOLD WING LABEL.

ANNIVERSARY WING LABEL. Notice the writing marking Red Wing's 75th anniversary.

SILVER WING LABEL.

Color Chart 1920s & 1930s

Brushed Ware
Dark Green
Blue Green
Light Green
Luster Green
Bronze Tan

Early Glazed Ware
Dark Blue
Light Green
Green – White Trimmed
White – Green Trimmed

Medallion Line
Ivory – Brown Wipe
Ivory – Green Wipe
Green – Brown Wipe
Yellow – Brown Wipe

RumRill
Pink
Matte White
Gypsy Orange
Aqua
Eggshell
Yellow
Aqua – White Lined
Ocean Green – Green Lined
Seafoam Ivory – Nile Green Lined
Dutch Blue – White Stipple
Crocus Green Gray – Pink Lined

Other Glazed Ware
Matte White
Blue
Pink
Green
Nokomis
Yellow
Green – White Lined
Matte White – Green Lined
Pink – White Lined
Coral – Tan Lined

Note: Although this does not include all the colors of this vintage, it gives a good overview of them.

Color Chart 1940s

Glazed Ware
Blue
Aqua
Matte White
Pink
Yellow
Green
Nokomis
Matte White – Green Lined
Pink – White Lined
Blue – White Lined
Ivory – Brown Wipe
Ivory – Green Wipe
Green – White Lined
Luster Blue – Coral Lined
Orange – Gray Lined
Tan – Green Lined
Maroon – Gray Lined
Dutch Blue – White Stipple
Gray – Yellow Lined
Luster Blue – Coral Lined
Orchid – Yellow Lined

Note: Although this does not include all the colors of this vintage, it gives a good overview of them.

Color Chart 1950s & 1960s

Glazed Ware
Matte White
Yellow
Gray
Cypress Green
Cinnamon
Black
Sagebrush
Hyacinth
Orchid
Coral
Blue
Salmon
Butterscotch
Bronze Green
Ice Green
Walnut Green
Cocoa Brown
Luster Blue – Coral Lined
Salmon – Yellow Lined
Coral – Yellow Lined
Blue – Yellow Lined
Lemon Yellow – Gray Lined
Matte White – Green Lined
Coral – Colonial Buff Lined
Walnut Green – Coral Lined
Forest Green – Yellow Lined
Light Gray – Pink Lined
Metallic Brown – Green Lined
Metallic Brown – Butterscotch
Maroon – Gray Lined
Gray – Yellow Lined
Gray – Coral Lined
Cypress Green – Yellow Lined
Cocoa Brown – Yellow Lined

Fleck Colors
Fleck Zephyr Pink
Fleck Nile Blue
Fleck Yellow
Fleck Green
Fleck Nile Blue – Colonial Buff Lined

Decorator Line
Crystalline Glaze
Blue
Silver Blue
Burnt Orange
Prismatique Line
Lemon Yellow – White Lined
Persian Blue – White Lined
Celadon – Mandarin Orange Lined
Mandarin Orange – White Lined
White – Mandarin Orange Lined

Belle Line
Olive Green – Moss Green Lined
Chocolate With White Overlay
Snow White – Orange Lined
Peacock Blue – Emerald Green Lined

Ashtrays
Silver Green
Burnt Orange
Radiant Orange
Metallic Brown
Caramel Gold
Orchid
Matte White

Note: Although this does not include all the colors of this vintage, it gives a good overview of them.

Index

Schroeder's ANTIQUES Price Guide

. . . is the #1 best-selling antiques & collectibles value guide on the market today, and here's why . . .

8½ x 11, 608 Pages, $12.95

- *More than 300 advisors, well-known dealers, and top-notch collectors work together with our editors to bring you accurate information regarding pricing and identification.*

- *More than 45,000 items in almost 500 categories are listed along with hundreds of sharp original photos that illustrate not only the rare and unusual, but the common, popular collectibles as well.*

- *Each large close-up shot shows important details clearly. Every subject is represented with histories and background information, a feature not found in any of our competitors' publications.*

- *Our editors keep abreast of newly developing trends, often adding several new categories a year as the need arises.*

If it merits the interest of today's collector, you'll find it in *Schroeder's*. And you can feel confident that the information we publish is up to date and accurate. Our advisors thoroughly check each category to spot inconsistencies, listings that may not be entirely reflective of market dealings, and lines too vague to be of merit. Only the best of the lot remains for publication.

Without doubt, you'll find
SCHROEDER'S ANTIQUES PRICE GUIDE
the only one to buy for
reliable information and values.

COLLECTOR BOOKS
A Division of Schroeder Publishing Co., Inc.